# THE CASE OF THE MISSING BLACKFEET WOMEN

*50 States of Crime*

NEW YORK: THE ALICE CRIMMINS CASE

CALIFORNIA: THE GOLDEN STATE KILLER CASE

OHIO: THE CLEVELAND JOHN DOE CASE

MISSISSIPPI: THE EMMETT TILL CASE

SOUTH CAROLINA: THE MURDAUGH MURDERS CASE

WASHINGTON, DC: THE CHANDRA LEVY CASE

MONTANA: THE CASE OF THE MISSING BLACKFEET WOMEN

# THE CASE OF THE MISSING BLACKFEET WOMEN

ANAÏS RENEVIER
TRANSLATED BY LAURIE BENNETT

CRIME INK

CRIME INK
NEW YORK

THE CASE OF THE MISSING BLACKFEET WOMEN

Crime Ink
An Imprint of Penzler Publishers
58 Warren Street
New York, N.Y. 10007



First edition

Cover design by Charles Perry, inspired by the French language edition cover design by Nicolas Caminade

Interior design by Lia Kantrowitz



Library of Congress Control Number: 2025935478

Paperback ISBN: 978-1-61316-738-0
eBook ISBN: 978-1-61316-739-7

10 9 8 7 6 5 4 3 2 1

Printed in the United States of America
Distributed by Simon & Schuster

# Contents

**PART 3**

**VENGEANCE (2020–2024)**



**APPENDICES**

To Loxie Loring, Kimberly Loring, Rhonda Grant-Connelly, Wilma Fleury, Carlene OldPerson, Paula Castro, Bettina Tallbull, Darlene Limberhand, Sherri Ewing, Ann Marceau, and all courageous mothers.

❖

*"We're Indian women. We have to deal with reality when they go off and play. And at the end of the day, we are the ones who make it work."*

**– RITA, *RESERVATION DOGS*, SEASON 1, EPISODE 4**

# PROLOGUE

## MARCH 2024, BROWNING, BLACKFEET RESERVATION, MONTANA

In this part of Montana, it can snow even in July.

At least, that's what the locals like to say, to paint a picture of their endless winters. After a brief spring thaw, the Blackfeet Nation is bracing itself for yet another late-season blizzard. In the distance, beyond the wind-scoured landscape, the Rocky Mountains stand, still blanketed in deep white snow clinging to steep slopes. In the sleepy town of Browning, the headquarters of the Blackfeet Nation, the rez dogs—stray canines that roam the reservation—seem numbed by the return of freezing temperatures. Dusty trucks fishtail over glaring patches of ice, weaving through potholes that grow deeper with every passing winter.

The people who live in this sovereign territory, which butts up against Glacier National Park, are equipped to deal with cold weather. There's a shovel in the back of every car or truck to dig out any drivers who might get caught in a storm. There's bear spray in every glove box, for the grizzlies just waking up from a long hibernation. And typically within arm's reach is a well-oiled gun, sacrosanct in Montana. Around these parts, carrying is a necessary precaution in all seasons. Because on the Blackfeet Reservation, crimes are like snowstorms. They catch you off guard and hit more often than you'd expect, in winter and summer alike.

"You know what they say: 'You want to get away with murder? Go to Browning.'" Three women sit together, talking. They live on the reservation and are gathered at their new headquarters in an abandoned downtown building to discuss one important item on the agenda: finding a way to fight crime. One of them is brewing a strong pot of coffee, or "cowboy coffee," as she likes to call it. She's well into her fifties, with sad, watery eyes. Her gait is slow, as is her speech, marked by a strong rez accent. She speaks like so many others who have grown up on Native reservations, with stretched syllables, a measured cadence, and a distinctive lilt.

All three are mothers. All three share the same accent and the same pain. A few years ago, they were mostly strangers, just familiar faces around town, or people whose names they'd heard of. That was before three tragic events, all so similar, bonded them for life. Around the table, they sip freshly brewed bitter coffee and pass around a roll of paper towels to dab at their eyes. They retell their stories, go over the facts, and play back the scenes in their minds.

Their tales are eerily similar. Within only a few years, each lost a loved one. A daughter, a son, a nephew. The cops were indifferent to their plight. Search parties were organized by the families, alone, out in the cold. And the bodies were found in the snow after a few days or weeks. Without a solid investigation, no one was ever arrested. But all three women are convinced they know who is to blame for the deaths.

One of them bursts into tears, and someone hands her a few sheets of paper towel.

Woman 1 says, "I think I'm gonna buy a gun. I'm about to lose it."

Woman 2 weighs in, adding, "It's not a bad idea to have a gun. You know, once, I almost ran down a suspect with my car."

Woman 3 admits, "I almost went through with it this one time. A guy raped my sister back in the day. I was out driving, and I saw him walking on the side of the road. There was no one around. No one would know."

She pauses to take another sip of coffee. "He doesn't know it, but he almost died that day. But we have more dignity than that. There must be other ways to get justice."

# PART 1
# VANISHED
# (2017–2018)

1.

# A BLACK CLOUD

Roy Lee HeavyRunner never did find out why his daughter Ashley was acting so strange on June 5, 2017. He'd rarely seen her so worked up. That day, when she showed up to his place, a small, gray wooden house in downtown Browning, she wasn't herself. She was nervous and told him twice, "I did something!" Frantically, she shut the blinds.

In the half-light, he waited, wondering if Ashley would eventually explain what was going on. But she was guarded and they sat in tense silence. From inside, Roy could hear the muffled hum of the reservation, the kids next door shouting, and the rez dogs barking. Suddenly, the familiar, comforting sounds were interrupted by the rumble of a vehicle pulling up to the house. Out of habit, he stood up and went to the window but pulled away when Ashley screamed "Don't look!" Then, in a flash, she sped off as quickly as she'd come in. The vehicle outside started up again.

A few hours later, the same scene unfolded about twenty miles away, where Ashley was living on her grandmother's ranch. She burst in, packed a few things into a blue backpack, then left in a flurry. From the window, her grandmother watched her get into a car. That was the last time any of her family members saw her—because Ashley Loring HeavyRunner vanished without a trace. That summer, some people within the Blackfeet community began to refer to her disappearance as a "black cloud," one that never really dissipated. Officially, no one even knows when or where she went missing.

By the time she was twenty years old, Ashley had inherited a certain vulnerability and dreams typical for girls her age. She was a young Native American, ready to give herself a fresh start, far from this place that was leading her nowhere. What did this rural, isolated territory in the backwoods of Montana have to offer her? Big skies, clean and crisp northern air, and grasslands as far as the eye can see. Memories of a childhood spent on her grandfather's ranch, looking after his horses. Summer days out bowhunting or swimming in rivers with friends.

But she also had to contend with the harsh reality of so many Native American reservations like hers. She lived in a place where houses were boarded up, condemned by the cops because they'd been used for dealing. The kind of place where, after dark, only the occasional pedestrian would stumble through, haggard, in an opiate stupor. The kind of place where homes were protected by hefty barbed wire fences, threatening guard dogs, and signs warning "video surveillance." Each fortified security system was a symptom of a life spent navigating dire statistics: above-average crime, unemployment, and poverty; a life expectancy that was far too short; and a high prevalence of alcoholism and drug abuse serving as a lifeline.

Ashley felt deeply connected to her ancestral lands but also felt condemned to them. She wanted to gamble on a different place only a three-and-a-half-hour drive away from that brutal existence. She and her sister Kimberly had promised each other they'd move to Missoula, a college town and a hub for writers in Montana. That's where Ashley would go back to school. She just had to wait for Kimberly to come home from a trip to Morocco, where she'd been visiting her fiancé for three months.

On June 8, 2017, at 10:25 P.M., Kimberly's plane landed at the Missoula airport. But when she checked her Messenger inbox, there was no news from her little sister. It was unlike Ashley not to check in and make sure her big sister had made it back safely. In the morning, Kimberly checked again and found that Ashley hadn't logged onto Facebook for eighteen hours. That was also unusual, but she wasn't overly concerned.

Of all their siblings, Kimberly was the levelheaded one. With her little sister, who was three years younger, it was a different story. She had this annoying habit of misplacing her phone or taking off for days at a time, without warning anyone. And lately, since their grandfather's death and after a rough breakup, Ashley had been pulling away from the family. She cried more, spoke less. She struggled with depression, then medication, hard drugs—especially meth—and was in denial about it. When confronted, she would swear "I don't have a drug problem."

But it was obvious she was on a slippery slope. Once so bright and joyful, a fiery girl with an infectious laugh, Ashley had become a different person. Behind her little rectangular glasses, her brown eyes had lost that sparkle. Lately, she'd lost weight. She'd always been slim, and was a star athlete in high school, but now she weighed only ninety pounds, at five feet, two inches. With Kimberly away these past months, Ashley had been going to more and more house parties and getting deeper into drugs. At only twenty years old, Ashley was being pulled into a drug addiction spiral, but there was still hope—in early June, she'd told her family she wanted to go to rehab.

So as Kimberly waited for a sign of life from her sister, she pored over old messages and reread their last text exchange from the evening of June 7, just before her return flight.

"Are you okay?" Kimberly had asked.

"Always, what about you?"

"Just packing."

"When you gonna be home?"

"Tomorrow night at ten. Are you home?"

"No."

Kimberly tried to reassure herself—if Ashley had needed help, she would've said something right away.

❖

Ashley's parents couldn't stop thinking about the last time they'd seen their daughter, playing back those final scenes in their minds over and over. They had separated when she was young, and each now bore the weight of their own guilt as they scoured the recesses of their memories, hoping to find a clue. Or perhaps absolution. They'd analyzed her every facial expression and gone over each of her last words.

Roy Lee HeavyRunner had been haunted by so many questions since Ashley stopped by his place on June 5, 2017, three days before she last logged onto Messenger. She'd told him she "did something." What had she done? And who had she left with?

Around that time, Ashley's truck had been out of commission for a while, so she did what she could to get around the reservation, which spanned more than 1.5 million acres, an area bigger than the entire state of Delaware. It could take more than an hour to drive from one place to another on the Blackfeet Reservation, and Ashley lived in a relatively isolated spot at the southern end of the territory, near the small town of Heart Butte.

She'd often shoot off a bunch of texts when she needed a ride, occasionally offering to pitch in for gas. Her friends would come by to pick her up. If only Roy Lee HeavyRunner had glanced out the window at that moment, he might have recognized the driver and held the key to solving this mystery.

We know after Ashley stopped by her father's house, she went back to her grandmother's ranch. Three generations of Lorings lived under her roof: Ashley's grandmother, her half siblings, and her mother Loxie Lynn, who everyone called Loxie. On June 5, Loxie wasn't home. She'd been away on a trip to Great Falls, which was two hours from the reservation, and hadn't given anyone a return date, saying she'd be back in a couple of weeks or so. Her last conversation with Ashley was on the day she left for Great Falls. Her daughter had asked to go with her, but Loxie said no. She hugged Ashley and told her she loved her.

When Loxie returned on June 12, she found Ashley's room empty, and no one in the house had heard from her. She immediately called the tribal police to report her missing. An officer said her daughter was of age and she might just be out with friends. But Loxie pushed back, explaining there'd been no sign of life from Ashley for days. Her pleas fell on deaf ears—the authorities saw no cause for alarm. Soon after they reported her missing, Ashley's relatives heard she might be staying with a family friend who lived in an area with no cell service.

When a few days later Roy Lee HeavyRunner went into liver failure and was hospitalized, she was still unreachable. Eventually the family friend came back into town, but he said he hadn't seen Ashley in a while.

This set off alarm bells. Now her loved ones were sure of it—something had happened to Ashley. Kimberly felt a surge of panic. It was time to make a few phone calls to get to the bottom of things.

If you disregard the text exchange between Kimberly and her sister on June 7, the last concrete evidence that Ashley was alive is from June 5, the day her grandma saw her for the last time. That same day, someone shot a video of a house party at the home of a man named Vernon, and Ashley appeared in the footage. The video was posted to Facebook right after the party, showing young people drinking beers, with Ashley sitting on a couch in the background. Though the video was quickly taken down, many witnesses told Kimberly they'd seen her sister that night.

They also told her Ashley had tried to hitch a ride home from the party, but her friends had turned her down because she was too "fucked up." So by the middle of the night of June 5 to 6, Ashley was left alone in

Vernon's home, obviously intoxicated and without any means of transportation.

Kimberly had no definite proof to explain what might have happened to her sister after the party. The precise timeline was still unclear, with so many gaps. And, especially, she had to sift through fragments of rumors and make sense of people's calculated silences. On this reservation with a population of ten thousand, everyone seemed to know everyone, which could have been an asset.

But then, everyone was suspicious of everyone else too. Ashley had also been running in some shadier circles, where a code of silence protected secrets about illicit activities. People tended to avoid pointed questions and dreaded the answers they might uncover. Convinced that someone knew something, Kimberly relentlessly posted on Facebook and contacted all her sister's friends and acquaintances, chasing after false information and solid tips. Eventually, it all seemed to point to a new lead, a house that has been the focus of several police investigations over the years.

The place had since been demolished, but at the time Ashley went missing, it was butted up against other trailers on a big property near the road into Browning. The tenant, thirty-eight-year-old Alvin Dog Taking

Gun, nicknamed Big Al, was known for two things that tended to be closely connected: He was on the police radar for his alleged involvement in drug deals and the kids on the reservation knew him for his house parties, which happened so often that people around town called his place "the party house."

On the night of June 6 to 7, 2017, there had been another party at Big Al's, and the event had been in full swing well into the early morning. No one can say exactly what Ashley was up to between Vernon's party on the evening of the fifth and this party the next day, but several witnesses stated she was at Big Al's place on the night of June 6. Had she been at the party when she sent those last messages to Kimberly before her flight back from Morocco? The timing seemed to line up.

According to one person who was at the party, Ashley had spent awhile in the kitchen chatting with a guy in his fifties who lived on the reservation. He was later seen leaving Browning in his truck with Ashley at first light on June 7. After that, she vanished into thin air.

❖

For members of the Blackfeet Tribe, the northern end of the reservation holds sacred grounds. Ninaistako, or Chief Mountain, inspired many creation myths and remains the focus of traditional ceremonies to this day. The mountain towers over Saint Mary Lake, a place with its own spiritual significance and tales of spirits haunting its shores.

As a result of negotiations with the US government in the late nineteenth century, the Blackfeet Tribe—once one of North America's most powerful nations—was able to retain control of these sacred lands. The colonizers subsequently secured a more favorable arrangement for themselves, as was their practice. As settlers systematically killed off the bison that served as the primary source of food for local Natives, the Blackfeet people found themselves starving and cornered. Under these desperate circumstances, they agreed to sell off a large portion of their land.

Two decades later, in 1910, the federal government used that same territory to create Glacier National Park. Even today, only a fraction of the park's economic gains trickle down to the Blackfeet Tribe. The government collects the park's revenue, while the Natives operate a single casino and hotel in Browning and a few campsites on Saint Mary Lake.

In peak summer, during the high season, tourists hike around the lake and wander through the area, driving along winding roads. For the rest of the year, it's pretty quiet along Highway 89, which runs from Arizona all the way to the northern tip of the reservation, where it meets the Canadian border.

About twenty miles south of the border, an unmarked dirt road cuts through a dense stand of spruce, fir, and larch trees with silvery trunks. The road runs parallel to Highway 89, squeezed between the highway and the lakeshore. It's easy to miss, but Ashley's mother Loxie can practically find the turnoff with her eyes closed. Driving along the dirt road, you can catch a glimpse of a few homes in the distance, then a cabin with a red roof, on the edge of Saint Mary Lake.

Loxie can't recall the exact sequence of events or precise dates, but she'll never forget how she felt when she learned the owner of this cabin might be the last person to have seen her daughter. A sudden dizziness and a desperate need for an answer washed over her. His name was Sam McDonald. He was the man who'd been seen chatting with Ashley at Big Al's house party, the person she allegedly left with. And as Kimberly once put it, Sam ran in "the drug world."

Sam McDonald was fifty-three years old, and his son went to school with Ashley. A cloud of rumors hovered over him about his lifestyle, his drug use, and the bad company he kept. And he's the first to admit he hit rock bottom when he started doing meth. He lived in a cluttered, half-renovated cabin, surrounded by countless piles of stuff. Outside, scrap metal and tools were scattered across the yard amid rusted-out vehicles and dismantled engines. Inside, he had mounted rifles on the wall next to a crucifix.

Loxie has lost count of the trips she's made back and forth from the Heart Butte ranch to this cabin, an hour's drive away. She's lost count of all the hours spent parked outside his place, tracking his comings and goings. All the times she fell asleep in her car, then woke up to Sam knocking on her window, telling her to get off his property. She was kind of obsessed. Most times, she insisted on going alone, without her children, because the man she was surveilling had a shady reputation. Loxie recalls how in the weeks following Ashley's disappearance, from her hideout, she saw plenty of girls come and go. Some were so much younger than Sam. She found it hard to believe that her twenty-year-old daughter could have been another one of his conquests.

Though Sam initially refused to speak with Loxie, things changed when, one day—worn down by swirling rumors and her dogged demands—he figured he had no choice but to tell his side of the story. It's a story that Ashley's loved ones have always taken with a hefty grain of salt.

Sam says that before the party at Big Al's place, he hadn't known Ashley; he'd just seen her around. They'd said hello to each other at a few parties, and that was about it. So the evening of June 6 would have been the first time they'd had a conversation. As Sam was heading out, he says Ashley asked him, "Sam, where are you going? [. . .] I don't want to be here." Then they left the party together to spend the night at his place, a lakeside cabin forty-five minutes outside Browning.

According to Sam, one night turned into almost a week, and Ashley ended up staying with him for five entire days. He said they drank and did meth the whole time they weren't sleeping. They spent the nights having sex and looking up at the stars. He said at one point Ashley danced by the lake, pointing at the sky. While she was staying with him, she also took off a few times. He never knew where she was going, but eventually she always came back.

On the fourth day, Saturday, June 10, Sam claims he drank so much that he collapsed, drunk, at around 5:00 P.M., just as Ashley was slipping out again. When she returned, at around one o'clock in the morning, she was "all fucked up" and Sam was sure "it wasn't meth." At that point, he thought it was time to get her home. He waited for her to come down a bit, then after another sleepless night offered to drop her off at her place.

So what happened next? He said Ashley balked at first but eventually accepted the ride. They hit the road on Sunday morning, June 11, 2017, and headed for her grandma's ranch near Heart Butte. In the passenger seat, Ashley typed away on her phone, then asked him to stop at a roadside pull-off about six miles from his place. Apparently, some guy she called V-Dog was supposed to pick her up there. Sam didn't know him. For all he knew, it could be a friend or a cousin.

So Sam claimed he parked his truck facing Divide Mountain, on a gravel pull-off that was out of sight of Highway 89. Next, Sam said, Ashley got out of the truck and sat on a log, staring at a cabin in the distance. She asked him how she could get to it. He said he wasn't sure but told her he thought a trail went around the back.

The next thing Sam remembered was waking up in the driver's seat.

He'd fallen asleep, and Ashley was gone.

## 2.

# BAD REPUTATION

Sam McDonald assumed he'd dozed off for just a few minutes. But when he looked at the time on the dashboard and saw the empty passenger seat, he realized forty minutes had slipped away, and Ashley too. As he tells it, Sam started to ask himself a lot of questions. Had Ashley disappeared with that guy V-Dog? Had she tried to go find the cabin they'd talked about before he passed out?

Had anyone seen Sam at the time, someone who could corroborate his story? Around midday on Sunday, June 11, a friend of Sam's, named Spoon, says he found him "confused and tired." According to Spoon, the two had spoken around seven o'clock that morning, when Sam suggested he come by so they could work on his vehicle together. But when Spoon arrived at 11:00 A.M.

as planned, Sam's son answered the door and told him his father was out and he'd have to come back in a few hours.

On his way home, Spoon crossed paths with Sam, who was out in his truck and appeared to be in rough shape, struggling in the intense summer heat. As Spoon recalls, it was over ninety degrees that day. He said Sam kept repeating himself: "I don't know where she went." He told Spoon Ashley had disappeared two hours earlier.

Two hours is a long time to be lost in that wooded, swampy, rocky terrain round the foothills of Divide Mountain; anything can happen in the vast Montana wilderness. It's easy to get lost, fall into a ravine, or encounter dangerous wildlife, like grizzlies, brown bears, mountain lions, lynx, coyotes, and wolves. Sam said he tried walking to the cabin Ashley spotted but couldn't get through the brush, so he drove around looking for her instead. In a later iteration of his story, he also claimed he saw people lurking around while he was looking for Ashley—two trucks, one blue and one brown. When asked if he could identify the drivers, he said, "No, I didn't recognize them. There's fifty thousand Indians out here."

It was an obscure tale told by an equally obscure character, and Loxie Loring was not buying Sam's story.

Relentless, she continued to stake out his place. Tensions rose, and Sam threatened her. "I've got cameras," he yelled. Loxie shot back that if there were cameras, then she wanted to see the footage of the day Ashley disappeared. But Sam refused flat out.

While Loxie was watching Sam, Kimberly was still running her own investigation, questioning their neighbors. She'd compulsively collected dozens of people's accounts, and their stories only made her more anxious.

Sam McDonald had neither the style nor the reputation of an ordinary, law-abiding neighbor. Broad shouldered, with thick calloused hands and a glassy stare, he wore a bandanna pulled tight around a long tangle of gray hair, topped by a too-small hat. He looked old for his age, the deep-set lines in his face bearing witness to years of drug use and alcoholism. His speech—made choppy by a strong rez accent and an upper lip twisted and frozen on one side—was slow, and his sentences dragged on as though weighed down by all the rumors that dogged him.

People were saying some girls had tried to run away from his place, naked, by swimming across the lake. Others had been seen in his yard with "syringes in their bodies." One woman claimed he built a secret room in his house and locked her in it. Another didn't provide details but wrote on Facebook that Sam "tortures women." The Tribal Council was notified that if they allowed Sam to keep living there and doing whatever he wanted, something bad was going to happen. And then there was that mysterious construction work that went on all summer after Ashley's disappearance. Loxie swears Sam tore out every bit of flooring in his place and completely remodeled his cabin.

There weren't many voices defending Sam. Even his friend Spoon's story was shaky, and while it didn't accuse him directly, it did nothing to absolve him. Spoon claims he crossed paths with his friend on a hot day, but, according to weather data from June 11, 2017—the day Sam said he dropped off Ashley—temperatures only got up to seventy degrees. On the other hand, it had been ninety degrees out between June 7 and 9. The fact was that regardless of how reliable their admittedly vague accounts were, neither man had bothered to report Ashley missing, not even to her family.

At this point, Sam McDonald was ticking every box and looking like the ideal suspect. But how did his story hold up against the town's universal passion, an obsession that thrives in all remote communities and rural villages? In short, how did it compare to the local gossip?

On Native reservations, sharing dirt was practically a national sport. Some Natives jokingly called it the "moccasin telegraph," which hearkened back to a time when people traveled on foot, wearing moccasins, and bearing news from elsewhere. Scandals were the perfect opportunity to settle scores through gossip and indirect accusations, even if it meant laying it on thick. On the Blackfeet Reservation, the rumor mill was running in high gear, and it wasn't about to pass up the mystery surrounding Ashley's disappearance.

Beyond the gossip, another cultural reality created additional layers of confusion in every statement about Ashley's disappearance. On Native land, the Western perception of time, seen as linear and hurried, still bumped up against a kind of natural resistance: "Indian time." Scheduling tended to be more elastic, time more circular. Stories were layered, told recursively through nested tales that blended past and present, without much concern for precise tenses. Dates and times were approximate.

The truth was hidden somewhere in between the inaccuracies and distortions. To grasp what each person stood to gain—and to uncover what they might be hiding—you had to come prepared, ready to read between the lines. In Ashley's case, some people's memories were muddled by drug use, further complicating the search for answers.

When you cut through the gossip and looked past all the holes in Sam's story, one question remained unanswered: If Sam did have something to do with Ashley's disappearance, why would he have opted to tell a story that made him an obvious suspect from the outset? He had a convenient alibi, sure, claiming Ashley disappeared while he was sleeping, in the middle of nowhere, far from any potential witnesses. But at the end of the day, it wasn't a solid explanation, instead casting even more doubts. If Sam truly was looking to hide a darker truth, he was a pitiful storyteller.

This begged the question: What if he was telling the truth? What if, in some improbable series of events, Ashley really had taken off while he was out cold? What if she left with that guy she called V-Dog?

After more than two weeks without any sign of life from her sister, Kimberly was still trying to cross-check statements. Fate had forced her to become a budding detective, and she scoured her contact list, hoping to stumble over a lead or some evidence. And she had her sights set on "the drug world." For a little less than a year, her cousin Tashina Running Crane had been seeing a man who ran in those circles. His name was Paul Valenzuela and he was fifty years old. So maybe Tashina knew something.

On June 26, 2017, Kimberly sent her a text. In a first message sent over Facebook, she asked a relatively innocuous question, the same one she'd asked dozens of people at this point: "Did you see Ashley?" An hour later, a reply came in, providing a hint and zero punctuation. Tashina seemed to be referring to Paul as her "ex-husband," although it's unclear whether they were ever officially divorced or even married. She wrote, "My ex-husband gave her a ride ask Paul Valenzuela he said he gave her a ride to cutbank [sic] a few weeks ago."

Cut Bank was a small industrial town at the edge of the reservation, connected to Browning by a straight stretch of Highway 2 and by a winding railroad that could get you from Chicago to Seattle in forty-six hours. The rail line ran one commercial load every hour and one passenger train per day.

Tashina added another sentence in which one or two words seem to be missing: "I'm sure she is trust me she's obviously a big girl." Then she admitted, "I'm mad at her."

Kimberly asked Tashina for Paul's number, which her cousin was quick to share, saying, "Keep me posted girl okay ill keep my eyes open."

Wasting no time, Kimberly texted Paul and asked, "Have you seen Ashley Loring? She is missing."

Paul's reply: "I got a phone call this morning asking the same thing. I know of her. Last I saw her was at clays famonds about a month ago. Sorry. But tashina is giving you false info. Ask her she prolly knows more than she's saying."

After being given the runaround by Paul and Tashina, Kimberly called one, then the other. Paul was angry and defensive. Tashina doubled down, claiming he knew something. Meanwhile, Kimberly was putting two and two together. She found out that Paul Valenzuela had a nickname. People called him V-Dog. So he was the guy who, according to Sam McDonald, Ashley had left with before she vanished for good.

Paul Valenzuela is a private person. There are no photos of him online, and he's barely on any social networks. Local journalists have been able to dig up only a few images, and they paint a picture. They are grainy black-and-white shots taken by law enforcement dashcams, like the ones recorded on September 3, 2016, when his white truck was pulled over by Washington State Patrol officers. In the video, the driver complies and steps out of his vehicle. It shows a man in a white T-shirt, with an average-to-slight build, a visible paunch, and a shaved head. He's chewing on something, looking indifferent, and seems to go along quietly. In the last few seconds of the video, he's sitting in the back seat of a squad car, cuffed, silent, and sullen.

His life—or V-Dog's life—can be described as a series of round trips: trips between the Blackfeet Reservation, where he grew up, and Seattle; and trips to and from prison and probation meetings for criminal charges—first an illegal firearms charge, then theft, burglary, and domestic violence. He became increasingly violent after his first arrest in 1986.

In June 2017, he was free but still as silent as ever. When Ashley's family contacted him, Paul was evasive. Tashina, on the other hand, provided long-winded answers. She had plenty to say about him, and Kimberly's phone lit up with a flurry of notifications. Tashina said she and Paul had gone to Seattle together around June 9. She didn't usually like traveling with him, but that time he'd insisted. She claimed they'd had an argument, started by Paul, after which he'd left her stranded in Seattle.

That was the evening of Saturday, June 10, the day before Sam said he gave Ashley a ride to the pull-off near Divide Mountain. Kimberly remembered this detail from when her cousin posted about her misadventure on Facebook. On June 9, Paul had reportedly told his parole officer about an upcoming trip, saying he planned to leave Seattle to head for Browning, Montana. That drive covers over six hundred miles and takes at least ten hours, if you stick to the speed limit and don't make any stops. It's exhausting, yes, but doable in one night. Plus, according to Tashina, Paul tended to drive fast and didn't take breaks.

She also said he didn't answer any of her calls that night after the fight. Could Paul have been on his way to meet Ashley the following Sunday morning? Was Sam's story actually believable?

Leaving town for three months means missing out on countless big life events, intimate chats, and minute details about your loved ones' daily lives. Before Kimberly went to Morocco, the two Loring HeavyRunner sisters barely kept any secrets from each other. But upon her return, Ashley's big sister was in for a few surprises. She learned Ashley had been Paul Valenzuela's mistress. People who were close to them confirmed the affair, and one of their uncles was very critical of the relationship. They'd first met around mid-May, and Paul had even gone to the Loring ranch bearing gifts. He'd brought a small medallion for Ashley's grandmother and gave the entire household a bundle of sweetgrass, a sacred plant traditionally burned in smudging rituals.

For Kimberly, this new information raised new questions. Could Ashley have willingly left with Paul? Could he have hurt her? Or could she be alive somewhere, with him?

By the end of June, while Kimberly was trying to get answers out of Paul—or at the very least some proof that her sister was alive—the family got a call from tribal law enforcement. Apparently, a witness had reported seeing a young woman running from a vehicle along Highway 89, not far from Divide Mountain and Saint Mary Lake. The girl looked just like Ashley.

3.

# KIMBERLY VERSUS THE GRIZZLY BEARS

Tragedy strikes at random, catching people by surprise. It leaves behind an audio reel etched into memory. The sound of an ambulance siren wailing in the night. The clap of helicopter blades slicing through the air. The voice of an operator asking, "Nine-one-one, what's your emergency?" An unremarkable family becomes a news story. A headline in the paper. A press conference. A media circus.

But for those living in the far reaches of a reservation tucked into a remote corner of one of the US's largest and most sparsely populated states, the story plays out differently. For Ashley, there were no sirens blaring, no roar of helicopters flying overhead. There was only Kimberly's voice echoing and fading out into the vast wilderness.

Although Loxie had reported Ashley missing a full two weeks earlier, on June 12, it took this tip to make Blackfeet police take the case seriously: A girl who looked like Ashley had been spotted running away from a vehicle on a desolate stretch of Highway 89, north of the reservation, in a swampy and forested area. Maybe it was finally time to send out a search party.

There was just one problem: The tribal police had eighteen officers on the payroll. On an average day, that meant the two or three officers on duty were responsible for covering the reservation's 1.5 million acres. As one former officer put it, decisions had to be made. "Let's say there are two or three of you on duty. Someone gets stabbed and then someone else loses consciousness forty-five minutes away. . . Where do you go first?"

Sometimes tribal law enforcement would get backup from the Glacier County Sheriff's Office or the Pondera County Sheriff's Office, as the reservation straddled both counties. But they, too, were often stretched thin. And then there was the Bureau of Indian Affairs (BIA) and the FBI. While the tribal police handled emergencies and petty crimes, the two federal agencies were responsible for investigating more serious crimes.

In late June, a search team was put together using whatever resources were available. An entreaty was sent out to the surrounding communities, inviting anyone who was willing to help to join the search for this girl who might be Ashley. A few BIA agents were dispatched to support the local effort, bringing along their own law enforcement team. Dozens of people combed the area, pushed their way through branches, clambered down to the Milk River, and climbed the steep paths toward Divide Mountain.

On the front line, Kimberly walked, disoriented and in shock. Instinctively, she called out her sister's name. "Ashley? Ashley? Ashley!" It was as though she expected Ashley to pop out from behind a tree or thicket. When Loxie heard her eldest daughter screaming, it made her ears ring and her head spin. She broke down for the first time since her daughter had gone missing. It was all too much, and Loxie crumpled to the ground. Kimberly's voice drowned out all other sounds: heavy footfalls on gravel roads, the dogs barking, the static bursts from the walkie-talkies, and hooves pounding the ground as riders sped out toward steeper terrain.

During the entire search, Kimberly never stopped calling Ashley's name. But all she heard in response was the hum of nature, alert and watchful. Insects flitted around budding flowers, and the air was thick in the heavy heat of early summer. At the end of the day, she headed home covered in mosquito bites, sunburned, and without any sign of her sister. The following day was the same. And the third as well.

Then volunteers came across a gray sweater left in an unofficial dump, amid garbage, barrels, and scorched tree trunks. It was in tatters, but Kimberly recognized it as one of her sister's sweaters because of the tiny hearts on the sleeves. An acquaintance confirmed that Ashley was wearing a similar sweater in the days leading up to her disappearance.

Kimberly wondered about another detail: The garment was covered with thick, oily stains. She remembered a rumor she'd once heard, so grim she'd tried to forget it until this point. Some people were saying her sister had been killed and her body had been stuffed into an oil drum. So Kimberly shared the information with law enforcement, and the sweater was packed up as evidence, taken away by BIA agents.

One more detail was that the sweater with the little hearts was found relatively close to Sam McDonald's place. And law enforcement never did release any information about the vehicle reported by witnesses, the one that had been chasing after a young girl along Highway 89.

The day after the search was conducted, tribal law enforcement finally wrote up the official report they'd been refusing to file since mid-June. Ashley Loring HeavyRunner, born November 23, 1996, in Browning, Montana, was now officially a missing person. Kimberly hoped this might be the start of an investigation.

Her hope lasted all of three days. On the fourth day, the authorities ended the search for Ashley. There weren't enough resources. They said sorry and good luck. Kimberly felt her heart shatter. With law enforcement nowhere to be seen, her father seriously ill, and her mother on the verge of a nervous breakdown, the twenty-three-year-old felt helpless.

In her solitude, she remembered a promise she'd made to her sister when they were children. She was eight at the time, Ashley was five, and the girls had been temporarily placed in foster care while their mother struggled with a drug addiction. They were afraid they'd be split up, so Kimberly had comforted her baby sister, saying, "We have to stick together. I'll always be there, and if you go somewhere, I'll find you."

Fifteen years later, with her sister missing and her mother using again, Kimberly told herself she had to stay strong; otherwise, nobody would be looking for Ashley.

In a Facebook post, she urged anyone who was willing to help to meet on Friday, June 30, at Milepost 21 along Highway 89. Horses were welcome, as the search area was immense.

At noon, a small group, which included one off-duty police officer, fanned out across the patchwork of surrounding trails. They soon came across another potential piece of evidence, a pair of boots that looked like the ones Ashley often wore, in her shoe size. There were dark stains on the leather. Could they be blood? The boots were handed over to law enforcement. But Kimberly had her doubts. They'd found the boots out in the open, on the ground right beside a stop sign, so she couldn't help but wonder if someone had deliberately put them there. With the next search parties, she stopped publicly announcing the specific dates and locations.

When she looks back on the days that followed, Kimberly mostly remembers a thick fog and a feeling of confusion. A kind of dissociation. "I had to make it in my head. It was not my sister. And that I was searching for a girl named Ashley. Because every time I knew it was my baby sister, I could not move."

Every morning, in a daze, she got ready and set off to comb the wilderness. In her backpack, she brought the essentials: bear spray and her Camel Menthols. As she once put it, "There's no tutorial explaining how to organize a search party." She learned the basics on her own over the first three days and figured everything else out on the fly. Loved ones in Portland helped from afar, using the satellite layer in Google Maps to find closed roads. Alone, with friends, and with family, Kimberly methodically checked out each one.

At the time, she weighed four hundred pounds, and the search was physically grueling. She would quickly become short of breath and moved slowly. But she stayed the course, walking for hours on end. Crossed rivers in her sneakers. Explored ravines. Dug where they came across freshly disturbed soil. Found animal bones a few times and had to determine whether they were human. Inspected an abandoned car riddled with bullet holes left out in a field. Plodded through swamps and pushed through krummholz, crooked trees deformed by icy winds.

In these landscapes, the walks became treks and her mission morphed into an obsession. Her greatest hope was also her greatest fear: She wanted to find Ashley, whatever the cost. In dense thickets, Kimberly dreaded the thought of tripping over her sister's body. So she made sure to call out Ashley's name, four times in a row, in a ritual known to attract spirits.

Ashley's mother Loxie went out with the search parties a few times before she opted to go it alone. On the days she felt up to it, she'd drive around to different spots. She'd spend hours parked outside Sam McDonald's cabin, then take long walks out in the wilderness, following random trails and searching for any sign of her daughter.

At forty-three, Loxie had a gentle face and a steely resolve—she knew full well the vast landscapes she was scouring were the perfect place to hide a body. One time, a smell stopped her dead in her tracks. It was the stench of rotting flesh, a whiff of death. Heart pounding, Loxie stepped off the trail, following the scent until she found a deer carcass in the underbrush. Then came the hush of leaves shifting in the trees behind her—a shape moved in the shadows. She froze as the broad head of a grizzly bear emerged through the foliage. Holding her breath, Loxie backed away, slow and steady.

In this part of the country, bears could be as big as a car. It's something a local guy had told Kimberly as a warning. But she couldn't have cared less. Those bears could growl all they wanted during the searches; she'd go rooting around in their dens if she had to. Who knew?

Maybe some grizzly bear had dragged away a piece of evidence, something belonging to her sister.

Then one day, a grizzly did chase down her little group of volunteers. They managed to get away from it in the woods, but they saw the near miss as a warning. "An angel was watching over us that day. We could have been eaten." Every time a search party went out, wild animals prowled the area, the sun beat down on the crew, and the heat was stifling.

Ashley's loved ones say that on several occasions they noticed trucks patrolling the area, like someone was keeping an eye on them. It happened so often, in fact, that they eventually developed a secret code to use over the walkie-talkies so the "bad guys" couldn't spy on them.

The woods were dark, the searches disquieting. Some volunteers threw in the towel. But Kimberly stubbornly kept on. "Everywhere I went, I seen Ashley. Any girl that would walk by, it was Ashley. I would look at somebody, and it would just be Ashley. And then when I, I would stop and look again, that girl wouldn't even look like her."

After a day out searching, she'd chain-smoke on the porch to quiet the anxiety that kept her awake every night. And every night, she came to the same conclusion:

She would never stop looking, even if it took her a lifetime. She knew that had the roles been reversed, Ashley would have stood her ground and demanded answers.

On the days Kimberly wasn't out scouring the local trails, she distributed posters with photos of her sister. She kept seeking answers on social media and, to collect even more people's stories, she created a Facebook page called "Find Ashley Loring/HeavyRunner." She cross-checked all the information, tallied up what she'd learned, and wrote down the names of those who knew Ashley but hadn't joined any of the search parties. In the list, she highlighted three names: Sam McDonald. Tashina Running Crane. Paul Valenzuela.

4.

# SASKATOON BERRIES

It was her dream job. In 2016, journalist Rachel CrowSpreadingWings began her career as a reporter, working at a local TV station called KFBB, in Great Falls. The city of fifty-nine thousand was the closest to the Blackfeet Reservation and famous for two things: the world's shortest river and an unusually high number of UFO sightings.

A year later, in the early summer of 2017, a series of social media posts caught her attention. Kimberly's posts were being shared by so many people that almost everyone in this part of Montana had heard about the disappearance of Ashley Loring HeavyRunner. But Rachel was surprised to notice that KFBB had not received a missing person report from the police.

Typically, when a family reported a relative missing, the police would pass on some information to the press, but in this case, there had been nothing but radio silence from the authorities. So she brought it up with her boss, explaining that someone had to be sent out to Browning, which was a two-hour drive away. For Rachel, this type of story hit close to home.

The Blackfoot Confederacy, or Siksikaitsitapi in Blackfoot, refers to a group of four nations—the Kainai, the Siksika, the Piikani, and the Pikuni—that straddle the US–Canada border, maintain cultural ties, and share a similar language and spirituality. Of the four nations, only the Pikuni are based on what is now US territory. In English, they are better known as the Blackfeet Nation or the Blackfeet Tribe. This was Ashley Loring HeavyRunner's tribe. The other three nations are located on reservations near Calgary, in Alberta, Canada.

Rachel CrowSpreadingWings was a member of the Kainai Nation, also known as the Blood Tribe. She told her boss that if Ashley had been a young rodeo queen from Kalispell, a predominantly White town near Glacier National Park, KFBB would have received multiple notices from law enforcement. She knew first-hand that the rules were different for people living on reservations. When her boss accepted the pitch, Rachel started by contacting law enforcement, but the person she spoke with didn't seem to find Ashley's disappearance concerning.

Next, Rachel interviewed Kimberly and aired her story. Eventually, forced to follow a news cycle that never stops, she had to focus on covering other events. But Ashley's case was always there, lingering in the back of her mind, until the day she had an unsettling encounter.

Rachel doesn't recall the exact date, but she remembers it happened when the Saskatoon berries were ripe. "It's a very Indigenous way of dating a story," she says with a laugh. She loves the sweet purple berries, which you can pick in early summer, so she'd scouted out a spot southeast of Great Falls. On one of her days off, Rachel parked her truck at a rest stop where Highway 89 meets Highway 87. She started picking by a small stream, with her headphones on, music blaring. In retrospect, she admits it might not have been her brightest idea, as a female out alone in a remote area.

Her basket was getting heavy when she looked up and saw a young woman standing within earshot. Rachel noticed another truck had parked next to hers, and a man was standing farther back in the parking lot. She and the girl exchanged a few words. The young woman was interested in her harvest and said she also used to gorge on Saskatoon berries when she was a kid. It was a polite, courteous interaction.

Rachel eyed the girl. She had dark hair, was quite thin, looked gaunt. Her white tank top was a little grimy and she seemed tired, like someone coming back from a long trip. Her hair was stringy, as if it hadn't been washed in a while. Rachel couldn't help but notice how much the girl looked like the missing person photos that had flooded her Facebook timeline just a few weeks before. The girl didn't seem to be in distress. If anything, she appeared a bit detached.

Although she found the situation unsettling, Rachel kept chatting, trying to act like nothing was wrong. She asked the girl where she was from. The girl told her she was from Washington and introduced herself. "My name is Ashley."

Rachel felt her heart skip a beat and thought back to her conversation with Kimberly, who'd shared one of her theories: Maybe Ashley had willingly gone to Seattle with Paul Valenzuela.

She glanced over at the man standing in the distance. Though she couldn't get a good look, Rachel figured he was about five feet, nine inches tall, and "definitely Brown." It could be him. She stood there, petrified. There was no cell service there. She was unarmed. She didn't know how to fight. She hadn't told anyone she was going berry-picking. If the man really was Paul, he could be dangerous.

Rachel weighed the pros and cons. "Do I risk him killing us both and dumping us in the river, or do I go back to my car and call the police?" And even if the girl really was Ashley, would she agree to go with her? She didn't dare ask any more questions; she didn't want to risk tipping off the stranger. So she offered the girl some of her berries and asked if everything was okay.

"Yeah, we just had a long trip," the girl explained. Then they said goodbye.

Rachel kept a straight face and pretended to go on picking berries. As soon as the couple's truck was out of sight, she sprinted back to her vehicle and rushed out to the nearest spot with cell service. She called the Blackfeet police, dialing the same number she'd used when reporting on the Ashley Loring case. The call lasted forty minutes.

According to the officer she spoke with, someone else had also reported seeing a girl who looked like Ashley in the small town of Augusta, just an hour and a half earlier. That was about the amount of time it took to drive from Augusta to the Highway 89 junction where Rachel had parked.

The officer asked her how sure she was that the young woman was Ashley. She wanted to say 100 percent. She'd felt it in her gut. And it was such a disturbing coincidence. But she backpedaled. On second thought, maybe it was 99 percent. Could she be wrong? Maybe she'd just panicked. What if she was accidentally filing a false police report and making trouble for a couple out on a road trip? The police reassured her, told her she'd done the right thing in calling, and said they'd look into the matter.

In the late 1990s, Paul Valenzuela's sister, Maria, learned how to hide a dead body. She didn't want to know how, and certainly had no need for the tip, but her brother, always keen to brag, shared it with her anyway. "I know how to bury a body. You put the body in first, cover it with dirt, and then you put a [dead] dog over it. So if cadavers [dogs] come and look, all they're gonna find is the dog's bones."

Maria described herself as different from the rest of her siblings. Over the years, she'd fallen out with her brothers; they'd dragged the family name through the mud too many times. She especially had a bone to pick with Paul because she claimed her "no-good, piece-of-shit" brother tried to sell guns to her teenage son. When she heard the initial rumors about Ashley's disappearance, she wasn't all that surprised that her brother's name had come up again. It wasn't the first time he'd been connected to shady business in some form or another. Worst of all, she had no doubt from the get-go that her brother could have hurt Ashley. She often wondered, "What else would a beautiful girl like her be doing with an old-ass man like him?" The answer: "Whoever's got the dope, man."

So Maria went to the police and told them everything: her fears about Ashley and the name of the kid her brother had buried twenty years earlier over some drug deal. Apparently, he hadn't killed the guy, but he'd wrapped him in a carpet and hidden the body somewhere in the mountains. Maria also took to social media to speak out. She was tired of Paul "getting away with his bullshit every time" and wasn't afraid of "a crackhead like him." There was no doubt in her mind that Paul had hurt Ashley. The police needed to check his phone records and nab him. At least that way, Ashley's disappearance would be an opportunity to see "fucking changes" on the reservation. Because Maria could see the writing on the wall. "If he keeps getting away with this one, it's never gonna stop ever."

And what did Tashina Running Crane have to say? She claimed that after spending some time in Seattle and after her argument with Paul Valenzuela over the weekend of June 10, he'd driven back out to Seattle to get her. Then she said they drove home around June 14 or 15. When they got to their trailer in Birch Creek, southeast of Browning, Tashina said, she no longer felt at home, that there was something lingering in the air, like the smell of decomposition. She explained, "There was something dead behind the house. I could smell it. Paul said, 'I don't know, one of the dogs is missing, maybe he's dead back there.'"

5.

# THE MOTEL BLONDE

The trailer home is a fixture of the American landscape, a cost-effective, prefab solution put forward by a nation struggling to address its housing problem. While it is ill-equipped to withstand natural disasters and the test of time, the trailer home does offer a cheap substitute to people living precariously—their own slice of an American dream worn thin. It is a roof over one's head, however flimsy or rusty it may be.

On the Blackfeet Reservation, most people lived in trailer homes and mobile homes built in clusters along the bumpy streets of Browning or scattered across vast grasslands. The trailer Tashina and Paul were renting back in 2017 looked just like the others, with weathered wood and tin siding, crooked windows, and a flat roof.

It stood on a big plot of land off a remote rural road. There wasn't much out there to disturb the peace and quiet, aside from another trailer a few hundred yards away, about a dozen guard dogs, and the quiet threat of a nearby forest thick with grizzly bears.

At twenty-nine, Tashina had a rounded face and hair that was often dyed blonde, with shifty eyes that seemed to hide a world of secrets. When she first noticed that "dead smell" in the backyard, she didn't try to figure out where it was coming from. She just accepted Paul's explanation that one of the dogs had died, and they went on living their life and getting into arguments.

Then, three weeks after Ashley went missing, while a summer powwow called Indian Days was in full swing on the Blackfeet Reservation, the police got another call. Paul and Tashina's trailer was ablaze. The fire was quickly contained, with only a small part of the kitchen sustaining damage. The culprit made no effort to hide. It was Tashina. When questioned, she told the police that Paul had just kicked her out, so she'd gone out to buy a few beers and fill up on gas—which got her thinking about revenge. Back at the trailer, she filled a bottle with gas and hurled it inside along with a cigarette. The fire ignited so fast she said she nearly lost her eyebrows in the process. After this umpteenth stunt, she moved out.

Over the following weeks, Tashina often messaged her cousin, Kimberly. She acted like she was looking for Ashley on her end too. But the truth was she'd stopped believing Paul's story about the dead dog. Now, she wanted to go back to his trailer and poke around herself. Her plan was to have one of her dogs smell a piece of clothing from Ashley and then sniff out a lead.

At first, Kimberly thought she'd found an ally and a source of information to help track down Paul. But Tashina was all talk and not much action, and her behavior was erratic. Kimberly often noticed her cousin's car near the areas they were searching, but Tashina never joined the search parties. And Tashina regularly drove by Kimberly's house late at night or early in the morning, as if she was patrolling the area. Was she looking for Ashley or surveilling Kimberly? She kept sending messages, accusing people, casting suspicion on Paul at times and then on strangers. She seemed to be everywhere, and yet she was always hard to locate. On her Facebook profiles, using pseudonyms, she shared several theories about what might have happened to Ashley.

Kimberly no longer had much of a relationship with her cousin, but she knew Tashina tended to act out when high or drunk. Sometimes she went off the rails. She had a habit of getting into spats and altercations over men. Tashina herself has confirmed this, and once said she "busted [a girl's] jaw with a pair of brass knuckles" in front of the C-Store, a gas station in Browning.

So Kimberly and Tashina stayed in touch and occasionally met to talk. Initially, they kept it friendly, perhaps to keep a better eye on each other. Then, one day, Kimberly noticed a gun under her cousin's car seat. The fact that she had a gun in the vehicle wasn't anything unusual in itself on the reservation, but Kimberly would think back to it later, when a new story emerged. Yet another story.

This time, a woman named Windy B, who lived on the reservation, was telling anyone who was willing to listen that Tashina had borrowed a rifle from her in early June—not long before Ashley went missing. And she'd never gotten it back.

When asked about the claims, Tashina responded that she didn't even know Windy and had no need to borrow a gun because she had her own firearms. She said she'd purchased every one, though she admitted most were stolen, so she'd eventually had to return a few to the original owners. She listed them all out: a .30-06 rifle, a pink butterfly .22 long rifle, a sawed-off shotgun, and a .27 or .29 caliber rifle.

And Paul had weapons too, she volunteered, saying he had "one of the loudest rifles in the world [. . .] and when it shot, it was like a boom!" Her answers were chaotic and bizarre.

Suddenly, she remembered Windy. Sure, yeah, maybe she had traded a gun for dope. Then she changed her story again and couldn't remember much because she'd been "higher than a kite" at the time.

As the summer of 2017 drew on, Kimberly began to have more doubts about her cousin. Around the time Ashley went missing, Tashina had been posting a lot on Facebook, starting with the weekend she claimed she was in Seattle. In this time period, she often posted her exact location online and provided detailed accounts of her arguments with Paul. This struck Kimberly as odd because she'd kept up with social media during her three months in Morocco, and Tashina hadn't published much at all in that time. She only started posting again once Kimberly was back in Montana. Why? Was she building an alibi? Did she have something to hide? And what about that fire early in the summer? Had she really started it in a fit of rage after a fight, or was she attempting to hide evidence?

One time, the two cousins were sitting together in Tashina's car when a line of police cars sped by, sirens wailing. Visibly upset, Tashina couldn't sit still and frantically dug around for her phone. She made a call in a panic but got voicemail. Her call was returned immediately, and Kimberly heard the person on the line say, "Don't worry, it's not about Ashley." She recognized the voice as that of Kenny B., a tribal police officer. Later, she would learn that he was also Tashina's lover.

For Kimberly, this was the final straw. The police didn't seem to care one bit about what happened to her sister, and now it turned out there might have been a bad apple in the mix, a corrupt officer. And this man was calling a person Kimberly deemed to be a suspect.

One day in August, she couldn't take it anymore and sent a message to her cousin. "Where is my sister?"

As always, Tashina launched into an incoherent, rambling explanation, saying:

"I think and believe paul has her me n u need to have dinner me n u are the only ones looking I got more info even a girl say on recording that she's ok"

"She's blonde"

"Paul's got her he divorced me"

"He moved to Seattle or there both in Shelby at motel 6 or fgunk [sic] but she's blonde now"

Kimberly asked her cousin how she knew all this, which car Paul was driving, and whether she had any proof, maybe a photo of her sister with blonde hair. Tashina told her there were no photos but a friend of hers had spotted Ashley at Walmart. They had a phone call, and Tashina was adamant: Ashley was with Paul, right now, at the Motel 6 in Shelby, a small town just an hour out of Browning. She even had the room number.

So Kimberly notified law enforcement, and a team was dispatched. At the motel in Shelby, officers did find Paul Valenzuela, and he was indeed with a blonde woman. But the woman wasn't Ashley. The woman in the motel with Paul was. . . Tashina Running Crane.

Years later, Kimberly still can't fathom why her cousin did that. For her, this was a point of no return. After the incident, she contacted the owner of the trailer Tashina and Paul had lived in and asked if she could search it. What Kimberly and a few community members found was a trailer that seemed to be under construction, looking as though it had been abandoned in a hurry. The space inside was gloomy, filled with a heavy silence disturbed only by the howling winds and the occasional distant growl of a grizzly bear. The walls had been hastily repainted and a section of the flooring ripped up.

Using the light from their cell phones, they searched for clues, moved furniture around, and sifted through the contents of several garbage bags. They noticed a discoloration in the carpet. Someone wearing plastic gloves used a box cutter to remove a piece, revealing concrete covered in a dark red stain. The little group of civilians stuffed the evidence into a plastic bag, along with some ammunition found at the scene and a pair of shorts Ashley's size. Then they handed everything over to the police.

By the end of summer, the two cousins were at war. On Facebook, Kimberly publicly called out Tashina. Tashina responded that she'd better talk to her lawyer and warned, "I'm going to sue anyone who points a finger at me!" She claimed she was the target of a "witch hunt" in Browning and posted a video on YouTube called "Set Up." Tashina recorded herself talking to a friend, explaining how she had been manipulated, saying, "Basically, he has Ashley. And everybody in this town knows it. Paul is trying to set me up."

A friend warned Tashina, "Because of your priors, because of your fucking fighting, you're fighting people up in public, you're shooting downtown, all of that shit, remember I told you a long time ago you need to stop it. They're banking on you being crazy."

The video was taken down soon after it was posted and, around the same time, one of Ashley and Kimberly's cousins received a new message. Apparently, someone named Rosie M. had made a confession, saying, "I had part in her murder." Rosie was a friend of Tashina's and the girlfriend of Vernon, the guy who'd thrown the party on June 5, the second-to-last night Ashley was seen.

Kimberly called her, and Rosie denied sending the message. She claimed her phone had been hacked. Could someone have sent the message from her phone while she wasn't paying attention? Was it a real confession? Or an awful prank? Who was taunting Ashley's family? In any case, this was the first time anyone had used the word "murder."

At this point, there were so many conflicting stories that only a police investigation could help untangle all these vague and disjointed accounts. But every time Ashley's family tried to contact tribal law enforcement or the BIA to find out how the case was evolving, no one returned their calls. After speaking with the cops, Paul Valenzuela's sister never heard from them again.

Journalist Rachel CrowSpreadingWings eventually found out the authorities never looked into the sighting she'd called in; in fact, there wasn't even a record of it. So she wrote a letter to her Montana senator, bringing to his attention both the investigation and how it was being conducted. As a precaution, she told him that if she were to go missing, it would not be of her own accord.

The weather was getting cooler, and things were slowing down. Autumn was settling in around the Rockies. Yet one thing had not changed: No one had heard from Ashley. Kimberly was still keeping an eye on Tashina, who eventually moved off the reservation. Loxie continued showing up at Sam McDonald's place unannounced—he was the last person to have seen Ashley.

Paul Valenzuela was more elusive, coming and going, but was eventually arrested in Washington State on illegal firearms possession charges. This time, he was going to prison. While Paul was incarcerated, he and Tashina got back together. This was now her opportunity to tell a new story, and blame Sam McDonald instead. According to Tashina, Sam had a solid motive to hurt Ashley; she claimed he was jealous of the girl's relationship with Paul.

Meanwhile, Ashley's sister Kimberly was done with these outlandish stories and put them all on notice: "They better speak up now because I'm going to make sure Ashley's name is everywhere. I'll make sure her story is gonna be huge. I just want to make sure they'll keep hearing Ashley's name. 'Cause I won't ever stop looking for her."

6.

# FIGHTING BACK

In Blackfeet culture, dreams are seen as profound and significant. They can be an omen or serve as a medium through which spirits convey messages. One morning, Kimberly felt her sister's presence by her side. In the dream she'd just awoken from, she'd found her baby sister in the mountains. Ashley had seemed happy and excited to see her. She'd introduced her sister to some friends, then showed her the way to a lake, where the water was clear and still, beneath a beautiful sky. A shooting star had streaked across the sky, and Kimberly had made a wish for her sister to come home. Ashley had said that her wish would come true.

Kimberly saw the dream as a sign that her little sister was saying to look for her around a lake. So Kimberly focused on the area around Saint Mary Lake, organizing about ninety search parties between June 2017 and February 2018.

In late fall, cold air rolled down from the glaciers, spilling across the plains. Winter had covered the Montana wilderness in snow and laid sheets of ice upon the roads, encouraging anyone in the area to stay inside. For Kimberly, it was an opportunity to take a break, though her downtime was punctuated by rumors and false leads that never stopped trickling in.

Her life, her future, had been turned upside down, and she spent most of her waking hours looking for her sister. She'd had to quit the new job she started when she got back from Morocco, then called off her wedding in Casablanca. Kimberly had put her entire life on hold. She lived off donations from the community and money from selling bracelets made by her relatives. Her grandmother organized a blanket dance, a traditional ceremony in which locals came to pray and give funds to Ashley's family.

Toward the end of winter, her relationship with law enforcement was at an all-time low. A spokesperson for the BIA was claiming they had conducted six searches, but Kimberly questioned their numbers. In fact, she had found these agents were spending more time at the casino than out looking for Ashley.

And then there was the long list of mistakes and inconsistencies. For starters, law enforcement claimed Ashley had officially been recorded as a missing person at the end of June, a full two weeks after Loxie notified them of her disappearance. But her name didn't show up in the National Missing and Unidentified Persons System, or NamUS, until November 14, 2017. That means that if during those five months, an investigator from another state had wanted to look for information about her, nothing would have appeared in the database.

Worse still was the misplaced evidence. What had happened to the tattered sweater smeared with oil and the red-stained boots found by a volunteer search party? They'd been lost somewhere between the many agencies—tribal police, BIA, FBI—involved, to some degree, in the investigation. When Kimberly found out about the missing evidence, she was livid.

With a renewed determination fueled by her anger, she contacted every local and national media outlet, one by one, casting bottles out to sea. In the local press, her sister's story drew little attention. When a few TV crews made the trip out to Browning, Kimberly struck a bargain: She'd provide an interview if they flew their drones over some of the more inaccessible areas she wanted to search. If she was going to find a clue or evidence, she had to jump on every opportunity, even the smallest ones.

In the interviews, Kimberly made it clear how she felt about the response from law enforcement. And when journalists contacted the different agencies and offices involved in the investigation to get their side of the story, they, too, were granted few answers.

In February 2018, eight months after Ashley was last seen, the FBI finally took over the case, perhaps in response to pressure from the press. Officially, they claimed it was because they would be following leads that went beyond the borders of the reservation, at the request of the BIA. It's hard to understand exactly how the BIA and the FBI, both federal agencies, decide who will handle cases that occur on reservations. Every investigation is assigned on a case-by-case basis, depending on agent availability, competing egos, and shifting alliances or rivalries in law enforcement.

Kimberly told the press the FBI's involvement gave her new hope, but her newfound optimism would soon be crushed yet again. A BIA agent told her, off the record, that the FBI wasn't going to look for Ashley.

Kimberly already suspected the case wasn't the FBI's number one priority because she sometimes went several months without hearing from investigators. But some bits of information about the investigation did eventually trickle down to her. Apparently, sixty interrogations had been carried out since Ashley went missing, and there had been several searches conducted at Sam McDonald's place. In an attempt to improve his image, Sam had changed his Facebook profile picture to a photo of Ashley. On social media, he boasted that he'd passed the lie detector test with flying colors. Tashina Running Crane did the same.

Meanwhile, Paul Valenzuela continued to serve his sentence in a Washington State prison. When he was contacted by journalists, he asked to be transferred to Montana in exchange for an exclusive interview, saying, "I'll even bring you where the people who did all this to Ashley are. Trust me, I am the only one who can do it." He declined to be interviewed after the press denied his request. No other potential suspects were named.

In a joint effort with the Blackfeet Nation Tribal Council, the BIA offered a $10,000 reward to anyone who would come forward with information that could help locate Ashley. The reward was later increased to $15,000. But nothing came of it.

Ashley's family and friends continued to criticize the authorities for their failures in the investigation, repeatedly stressing the fact that precious time had been lost in the first few weeks. Everyone knew the first days were critical in a missing person case. Because Ashley's family wasn't well off, because she was vulnerable, and because she was Native American, their cries for help had not been taken seriously from the start.

Kimberly continued to speak out on behalf of her sister, and on the reservation, where the community was constantly exposed to news about the case, a feeling began to take hold. Ashley's disappearance and Kimberly's dogged efforts had stirred up a growing fear and prompted a simple realization: No girl was safe from suffering the same fate.

Before he set up shop in a disused hangar in the middle of Browning, Frankie Kipp first had to negotiate with the spirits. The building sits next to one of the city's oldest cemeteries, so he had a few ghosts to chase down.

Frankie is about fifty years old, and he always says a prayer and burns sage to clear the space before entering. A man steeped in religion, he carries two sacred objects for spiritual protection: sweetgrass and a large gold cross bearing a crucified Jesus that he wears around his neck.

And—because you can never be too careful—he rarely leaves the house without his pistol.

Frankie learned to throw punches in Seattle's dive bars back when he had long hair and dreamed of a Native uprising and fight for civil rights in something like the American Indian Movement. After getting involved in a few too many tussles with White supremacists, he made his way out to the reservation to live a quieter life.

Putting bar fights behind him, Frankie turned to competition and amateur championships. He founded Blackfeet Nation Boxing Club in the early 2000s to provide an alternative to violence and drugs for the local youth. While the club turned out a few regional champions over the years, it didn't attract many girls. Until the 2017–2018 season.

At the start of the 2017 school year, one female teen started training at the club. Then another. By the end of the school year, there were about fifteen girls regularly coming in to train. Each was driven by the same fear that she, too, might vanish into thin air.

Ashley's face was plastered all over town, and her friends and family had put up posters of her in every school. Her name was on everyone's lips, her story brandished like a threat by parents trying to keep their children in line. She floated over the reservation like a specter, a "black cloud."

One of the new recruits that year was a girl named Serenity. She admitted she'd been afraid to walk alone on the reservation since one of her sisters was raped. Another teen, Mamie, said her grandmother had suggested she sign up. "She didn't want me to go missing like Ashley."

Even Frankie's own daughter, Donna, realized she could be next. Sitting in a semicircle in front of the ring, the budding young boxers took in Frankie's advice under the watchful eyes of Muhammad Ali, local boxing legend Billy "the Kid" Wagner, and a Native American man wearing a feathered headdress with the caption "Grandpa says no to meth!" Some of the girls were barely six or seven, wearing sparkly sneakers, pink sweatshirts, and gloves that were far too big for them.

When Coach Frankie spoke, his words were as quick as his punches in the ring, and he began each session with stories, like the one about his ancestor killed during the Marias Massacre perpetrated by White settlers during the Indian Wars, or the one about his grandfather, the "first Native millionaire on the reservation," poisoned by White men who allegedly changed his will so they could get their hands on his fortune. "They almost killed us all, so be proud of who you are, be proud to be Blackfeet," he lectured. With the girls, he hammered this point home: "If you don't fight for your life, you won't have a life to fight for." He asked them, "What should you do if someone grabs you?"

One little voice piped up with "Fight back!"

"Fight back, why?" said Frankie.

"So we don't get stolen."

Frankie Kipp, a former welterweight, has a unique perspective on boxing. He sees it as a sport, a challenge, a noble art. But also as an opportunity to respond to a visceral need to survive. Native Americans tend to be marginalized and life is not kind to them, both on and off the reservations. For Native women, it's even worse. So in between sets of push-ups, he taught the little girls with sparkly sneakers how to break an arm, how to give someone a nosebleed, and even how to gouge out an eye. "Jab, jab, throw your jab, an arm's length away, then aim for the nose. If he's bleeding a lot, your attacker will stop."

They say there are five seasons in Montana, the fifth one slipping in between a long, endless winter and a spring that struggles to get established. It's a sleepy, muddy season that stretches on. In 2018, it seemed to last forever. Mild weather finally made a timid and tardy comeback in May but didn't return in full force until June. A full cycle of seasons had gone by and Ashley Loring HeavyRunner was still missing. No progress had been made in the investigation, and the many law enforcement agencies involved couldn't seem to agree on anything. On their websites, each posted different dates and locations for Ashley's disappearance.

Around mid-June, Kimberly led a walk through the streets of Browning. One of her half sisters was at the front of the rally, on horseback, accompanied by the sounds of tribal songs and pounding drums. Kimberly was right behind her, looking grim, as she unfurled a banner with Ashley's name on it. In the second row, her mother Loxie held up a sign saying "We won't give up." A few girls from the boxing club had also been keen to join them. Other signs read "Where is she?" and "Protect our future!"

With her arms up, Kimberly brandished a sign that read "Break the silence!" She began to chant, repeating three names over and over again: "Sam! Tashina! Paul!" She had promised she would never leave them in peace, and she intended to keep that promise.

7.

# THE NIGHTMARE THAT NEVER ENDS

At the gathering Kimberly held for her sister in June 2018, two Blackfeet filmmakers joined the small crowd, cameras in hand. Ivy and Ivan MacDonald, sister and brother, were distant relatives of the Loring HeavyRunners. Ashley's disappearance echoed their own family story, a traumatic memory that was dredged up when they dug into the archives.

It happened on December 17, 1979, when their aunt Melba Theresa Wells went out to buy her daughter, seven-year-old Monica Still Smoking, a bicycle. Melba was particularly excited and happy that day because the family could barely afford that kind of gift. That Christmas was going to be special. But Monica never got to unwrap her present. She didn't come home from school that day. And although she knew the route well and had walked it many times on her own, she vanished without a trace in the middle of a snowstorm.

For two weeks, her family coordinated search parties, until a hunter made a grim discovery in the mountains of Glacier National Park, roughly twenty miles from Browning. It was a little girl's boot. Monica's body was found nearby, frozen in the snow. Her remains were sent to Great Falls for an autopsy, where the cause of death was determined to be hypothermia. But how could a seven-year-old girl have ended up so far from school, left alone out in the snow? It took the FBI two weeks to get to Browning and launch an investigation. The family never got answers, and no suspect was ever arrested or brought to justice.

Growing up, Ivy and Ivan had often heard relatives reminisce about this absent cousin with minnow eyes—one green, the other brown—but no one had ever mentioned the trauma surrounding her disappearance.

Ashley's case was making these kinds of stories come back up to the surface. Stories about girls who'd disappeared, families who'd gone out looking for them alone, and cops who didn't seem to give a damn. In the past, it had happened more quietly. But Kimberly now wielded the power of social media. How many girls had gone missing between Monica's and Ashley's disappearances? How many investigations had been botched?

This was the starting point for the two filmmakers. Wanting to talk about Ashley and Monica, they set out to make a documentary and called it *When They Were Here*. Soon they would find they had no choice but to add more stories to their film.

In the 2016–2017 school year, Ashley Loring HeavyRunner was a student at the local Blackfeet Community College. One evening, when she came back to the ranch, she couldn't hide how upset she was about her latest assignment. She quickly confided in Kimberly that she'd just learned that across the border in Canada, many Indigenous women were disappearing, and no one seemed to care. The authorities didn't appear to be looking for them, and Ashley wanted to "do something to help."

Since the early 1990s, activists—bereaved mothers, sisters, aunties, and daughters—had been sounding the alarm to Canadian authorities about the disturbing rate of unexplained disappearances and unsolved murders of Indigenous women on Canadian reservations.

Thousands of women had just up and vanished, at least forty of whom disappeared along the infamous Highway of Tears, which spans four hundred and fifty miles. After more than two decades of this activism, around the same time Ashley went missing, Canada was just beginning to grasp the extent of the crisis. And the movement had barely begun making its way over the border.

Senators Jon Tester, a Democrat, and Steve Daines, a Republican, were in diametric opposition when it came to their politics, but they formed a united front on one issue: Both Montana representatives served on the federal Senate Indian Affairs Committee, which oversaw matters related to minority "American Indian, Native Hawaiian, and Alaska Native peoples."

After days spent shouting herself hoarse, searching for her sister in forests and in mountainous terrain, after chanting the names of the suspects at rallies and powwows, after flooding social media with her messages, Kimberly's voice finally carried all the way into senate offices in Washington, DC. In response, Daines and Tester invited her to come testify in the Capitol. This would be her opportunity to air her grievances regarding the BIA and FBI.

Kimberly Loring HeavyRunner has a stutter. It might not seem all that relevant, but it's just one more hurdle she has had to overcome in every interview. There's always a moment when she lingers on a word and stumbles for a moment. Yet on December 12, 2018, she spoke with calm and gravity, as if she had surmounted her personal challenges to achieve this important mission.

The agenda was packed that day. Senators Tester and Daines wanted to draw attention to the recurring issues plaguing Montana reservations, and the list was long: Law enforcement agencies did not take violence against Native women seriously; there weren't enough police officers in rural Native communities; and there was insufficient communication between the various law enforcement agencies involved, which hampered investigations. Plus, law enforcement did not keep families informed of the progress in the investigations. The Ashley Loring HeavyRunner case was just one chapter in a thick book.

And Kimberly was not alone in what she called a "nightmare that never ends." She'd been invited to speak because her sister's story illustrated all the ways in which the system failed Montana residents when they desperately needed help. In front of witnesses, she went through her timeline and everything she'd had to do over the past eighteen months. On the stand, she recalled lonely searches, the lack of response from law enforcement, the affair between one tribal police officer and a suspect, lost evidence, and encounters with grizzly bears. She also told the story of Monica Still Smoking, the little girl found dead in the late 1970s, to highlight how, even then, the authorities weren't doing their job.

Senator Daines went on to bolster her testimony with hard data. At least twenty Native women had reportedly gone missing in Montana in 2018 alone, but only one had been found. He spoke of an epidemic of violence, a silent crisis, and accused the authorities of washing their hands of it. "I just wonder, if you would have had to kill a grizzly bear in self-defense, would there have been a more rigorous investigation of that incident than the investigation into Ashley's disappearance?" he speculated. "It raises a fundamental question about us as a nation, what value we place on human life."

Kimberly then told a story that drove his point home. One time, in Browning, when a deer was poached, fingerprints were found on the body and sent to a lab that same day. Meanwhile, she was still waiting for Ashley's sweater and boots to be analyzed. It appeared that elk were better protected than Native women. She concluded with "If they would've taken her seriously as a person, because we are important, I believe that my sister would have been here or we would have closure. We will no longer be the invisible people in the United States of America."

On the stand, a BIA agent was pressed to explain the situation. He was evasive, reluctantly acknowledging that the protocols around cases of missing or murdered Native American women needed some improvement. Next, a confused FBI agent reported that they'd found Ashley's body. The audience was stunned—Kimberly was in shock. But it turned out the agent had mixed up two cases.

What little trust Kimberly still had in the FBI was shattered that day. "They abandoned Ashley," she said, facing the committee.

It's amazing what a nationally televised testimony can accomplish. Kimberly had just left the hearing when she ran into a BIA agent who told her he'd made a call and located the sweater as well as the other misplaced evidence. Another surprise came the next day, when the

FBI claimed to have found human bones at the southern end of the Blackfeet Reservation. In a press release, they announced that the remains had been found and that the FBI, BIA, and Glacier County Sheriff's Office were working together to recover them. Evidence had miraculously been found, a skeleton was miraculously unearthed, cooperation between law enforcement agencies was miraculously established . . . And Kimberly was eager to get answers. Could it be Ashley?

Once again, her hopes were crushed almost instantly. It turned out to be a false alarm, as the bones were those of a policeman from the late 1800s. The search for Ashley resumed. Meanwhile, over four hundred miles away, another tragedy was unfolding, the story eerily similar.

# PART 2
# HYPOTHERMIA
# (2018–2020)

1.

# TWO SIDES OF THE STORY

The "red devils" had dared to stand in the way of the settlers and interfere with the gold rush. It was time to put an end to them. On a sunny day in 1876—on June 25, to be precise—Lieutenant Colonel George Armstrong Custer and his cavalry launched their assault on a Native American encampment. But things did not go as planned.

It became one of the most mythologized events in the history of the United States, retold through countless works of literature, film, and art. Most US citizens know—or think they know—what happened that day by the Little Bighorn River.

A few years earlier, gold prospectors had discovered ore deposits in the Black Hills, the sacred territory of the Lakota Sioux and Cheyenne peoples in present-day South Dakota. Miners swarmed onto lands that had been ceded to the tribes through a treaty and attempted, albeit unsuccessfully, to buy them back. What came next was a bloody conflict called the Black Hills War.

In late June 1876, eight thousand Native Americans gathered in southeastern Montana for a Sun Dance ceremony. These were free peoples who had fled systematic starvation on reservations in neighboring states and rallied around two Lakota chiefs: Thathánka Íyotake, better known as Sitting Bull, and Tȟašúŋke Witkó, or Crazy Horse.

On that fateful June 25, Custer struck, but the Lakota, Cheyenne, and allied tribes crushed his forces, decimating the troops and killing Custer himself. Never before had Native Americans inflicted such a devastating defeat on the United States. The country, still reeling from the Great Depression of 1873, needed a hero—so Custer became a mythical figure for this fledgling nation.

The Americans called it the Battle of the Little Bighorn, while the Natives called it the Battle of Greasy Grass. Two names for two sides of the same story. In one version, Custer was a martyr who had given his life for his country; in the other, he was a vain fool who'd charged toward his own death.

For decades, historians dismissed the accounts of the Natives who had been on the front lines. It didn't matter that they were the only survivors; their stories were deemed unreliable, their point of view erased from the official record. In the years that followed, the last free Native Americans of the Northern Plains were hunted down, forced to surrender, and shipped off to reservations.

Writer James Welch, born to a Blackfeet father, spent his childhood in Browning. In his 1994 book *Killing Custer: The Battle of the Little Big Horn and the Fate of the Plains Indians*, he set out to tell the story from the Native American point of view. He painted a picture of a Montana that was quite different from the one where he grew up, because the Little Bighorn battlefield sits near Wyoming and Yellowstone National Park, over four hundred miles from the Blackfeet Reservation. In this part of the state, far from the majestic Rocky Mountains, America's Great Plains fill the landscape: flat horizons, wide-open spaces, alfalfa fields, sagebrush meadows, grain silos, ranches, roads without any bends, run-down mining towns, and small valleys. A monument to the Little Bighorn battle was built on what is now the Crow Reservation.

Ironically, although these sworn enemies of the Lakota did fight in the battle, they did so on the side of the settlers. Today, their reservation is one of the largest in the United States, with a footprint five times greater than the Northern Cheyenne Reservation next door. Yet both tribes have roughly the same number of residents. To this day, the Crow and Cheyenne tribal members love to hate each other, but as neighbors, they've learned to face the challenges that come with life on a reservation together. In this desolate part of the country, it can be hard to imagine how these were once bitterly disputed lands of plenty.

And what of the Black Hills gold that started it all? In the late nineteenth century, the sacred mountain range became the property of the federal government. People say you can still find gold in the surrounding streams. The local legend has even become a tourist attraction, drawing in travelers who pay a $14.95 entry fee to pan for gold they know they won't find.

Author Jim Fergus once wrote that according to the Cheyenne people, everything that once happened on the land continues to exist within the land itself. At Little

Muddy Creek—the site of a lesser-known battle in the Black Hills War—the earth remembers blood and violence. Here, another girl went missing in December 2018.

In the days leading up to Kimberly Loring HeavyRunner's testimony before the Senate in Washington, DC, Henny Scott vanished into thin air. She was fourteen years old, with a round face, leading a normal teen life. Living on the Northern Cheyenne Reservation, she had big dreams. Henny wanted to be a doctor one day to advocate for Native Americans neglected by a fragile health care system.

On December 8, 2018, she went out with some friends after basketball practice. They headed for a remote house up in Muddy Creek, where teens from the reservation liked to hang out and party. Once there, Henny called her mother, Paula Castro, from the landline to let her know where she was. But Paula didn't like her daughter spending time out there and told her to come home right away. Henny said okay, but hours later, she still hadn't shown up.

So her stepdad drove out to the party house, where another teen told him Henny had walked off on her own. This surprised him because she wasn't the type to just up and leave.

Her mother filled out a missing person report with tribal law enforcement, then did the same with the BIA in Lame Deer, where Northern Cheyenne tribal headquarters are also located. She says it felt like they weren't taking her seriously. The officers and agents she spoke with shot back with their usual responses, suggesting Henny was still out partying or had gone off with a new boyfriend. They told Paula her daughter had probably just run away—if she had, it was probably because she was too scared to come home.

Temperatures were below freezing, and Paula realized the cops were not going to help her. So her family printed posters with Henny's photo, while volunteers from the Crow and Cheyenne reservations organized a search party. Leading the search efforts was Lame Deer resident Theresa Small, the Tribal Council's disaster and emergency services coordinator. This wasn't the kind of crisis she was trained for, but she tried to apply what she knew to the search for Henny, despite having to work with what she bitterly describes as "third-world resources." "We're a nation within a nation," she explains. "Things don't move at the same pace here." Small rounded up riders and asked around for search dogs, then dozens of volunteers got to work combing through sagebrush, searching every thicket.

Soon after her daughter's disappearance, Paula had a premonition. Deep down, something told her Henny was no longer with the living.

After weeks that felt like a lifetime, her gut feeling was confirmed. It was December 28, and it had begun to snow again after a brief thaw in a harsh winter. The tragic news came with the return of the cold, and FBI agents were dispatched to the Muddy Creek party house.

Henny's stepfather rushed out to the scene. He knew she was gone as soon as he saw the FBI agents. Twenty-one days after his stepdaughter went missing, her body was found less than two hundred yards from the party house. "You could see the house door, the fucking door, a straight shot from where she was laid," he later explained. Her body had been right there, right under their noses.

The coroner's report came in a few days later. It stated that Henny Scott had been drinking. Officially, she'd died of hypothermia.

"She froze, and here's her clothes. You want us to dry-clean them before you pick them up?" That's more or less how a police officer delivered the news to Paula Castro. She refuses to believe her daughter—even if she was drunk—just left the house, lay down in a field, and let herself freeze to death. She wasn't wearing a coat, so was she running away from someone?

Her parents wonder about other details too. She had a bump on her forehead, and there were bruises, scratches, and some kind of burn on her body. It looked like her nose was broken. And, especially, how could it be that none of the search teams came across her body in the three weeks they spent combing the area? Had someone left her body there later? These questions haunted Paula as she buried her child, the second child she'd lost. Henny went into the ground next to her brother, Charlie C.J. Scott, who committed suicide in 2014.

When the local press covered her story, they cited Paula's skepticism about the official cause of death. On January 9, which would have been Henny's fifteenth birthday, her loved ones organized a march to demand answers.

Jon Tester, one of the senators who had invited Kimberly to speak in Washington, wrote a letter to the directors of the FBI and BIA less than a month after admonishing them in Congress. He criticized the authorities for failing to do their jobs and condemned their "delayed, ineffective responses" on reservations, calling the problem "systemic."

Some parts of a bear skeleton look just like human bones. In fact, the resemblance is striking. It's one of the basic lessons Cary Lance learned while searching for bodies in the wilderness. He's gotten them mixed up before and figures there's a reason Natives call these animals "brother bear." Cary speaks Crow, practices the tribe's spirituality, and has lived on the reservation since 1969. But, as a White man, he's a bit of an exception in this place.

He was seven years old when his parents opened the first gas station in Pryor, a village in the west end of the immense Crow territory. To help him fit in, tribal Elders gave him his own Native nickname, calling him White Buffalo. After twenty years spent serving his country in the military, he returned to the reservation in the early 2000s to take over the gas station after his father's death.

Around the same time, on September 18, 2004, his friend Robert "Bugsy" Springfield disappeared while out on a hunting trip. A small group set out to find him, led by Cary. He recalls "dirty, complicated" searches "out in the mud," exploring deep ravines, walking far out into the wilderness, and venturing into remote areas "where it would be easy to hide bodies." Cary chased false leads and came across animal bones until winter rolled in, bringing with it an impenetrable wall of snow. After the cold season, some sporadic search parties were organized.

Then a rumor got them tracking down a new lead the next fall. They were looking for a suspicious abandoned car. The vehicle had tinted windows and a scorched passenger seat, with a deer carcass stuffed in the trunk. Not too far from the car, the search party came across bones, and this time they were human. They recognized Bugsy's jacket too. It had tears in the back, which, at first glance, looked like bullet holes or the work of a mountain lion.

When the FBI arrived, they put forward a preliminary explanation: A tree had likely fallen onto the victim. It didn't fit with what the group had seen, but who cared, really? Law enforcement went on to keep the body for three years before returning it to the family. They never provided an official cause of death.

In the endless search for his friend, Cary learned three things. One, you couldn't count on the police in this part of the country. Two, rumors on the reservation always had some truth to them; they were a way of speaking up for those who feared retribution and didn't dare come forward. And three, when someone went missing, you had to act fast, before the evidence was erased.

He appointed himself as the go-to guy for missing person searches, and he got himself a walkie-talkie, a waterproof camera, and eventually a drone.

So, of course, when Henny Scott went missing on Cheyenne land nearby, Cary went out to help. He flew his drone over the area around the party house, but the battery died just a few dozen yards from the body. "If it hadn't been for that, I could have found her. But sometimes, higher forces come into play. Sometimes the dead don't want to be found."

Cary was one of many people who believed Henny Scott's death was no accident. He drew his own conclusions from the local gossip. What he heard was that someone had beaten Henny up, and then, once she was knocked out in the snow, she'd been too weak to get up again. "If [the perpetrators] hold out long enough, they know everything will kind of dissipate, calm down."

With a Glock 19 on his hip—he never left the house without it—and a walkie-talkie perpetually close at hand, Cary was the kind of man who was always ready. But as 2018 drew to a close, he could never have anticipated the rate at which bodies would turn up over the following months.

# 2.
# THEN SELENA DISAPPEARED

Hardin was a small rural town like so many others in Montana. At the local diner, the burgers were good and greasy, while life outside was both harsh and monotonous. If you went by the number of churches in town—twenty houses of prayer for thirty-eight hundred souls—you might assume that some part of the community had found comfort in God, be it among the Mennonites, Lutherans, Adventists, Baptists, or Jehovah's Witnesses.

The only other local place to hunker down was the downtown casino bar and lounge. Tinted windows kept the dive in perpetual darkness, protecting whatever went on inside, which consisted mainly of a little cash changing hands, heavy drinking, and, around the sticky counter, dysfunctional behaviors and racist comments from unabashed Trump supporters.

But there was one thing that set Hardin apart from all the other remote towns in the Northern Plains: It sat in a county that had elected a Democrat in the latest elections. In a state that had always been a Republican shoo-in, this was an anomaly. There were only a few blue counties in all of Montana, and they included all of the state's eight official reservations. In Hardin, 40 percent of the population was White, and 50 percent was Native. Discrimination was pervasive, a daily occurrence in this town, and the problems that the Crow and Cheyenne tribal members experienced on the reservations spilled over into neighboring Hardin.

On August 29, 2019, a jogger was running down Mitchell Avenue, one of the town's main thoroughfares, when something strange caught his eye. In a backyard nearby, crows were circling above a pile of debris. The passerby thought he spotted something that looked like a body, so the Big Horn County Sheriff's Office was called in. On location, officers confirmed they were looking at the remains of a teenage girl decomposing in the stifling summer heat. After a quick investigation, the police were unable to identify the remains. On official documents, she became Jane Doe.

And yet a family on the Crow Reservation had been actively searching for their loved one for five days. On August 24, Kaysera Stops Pretty Places had gone out to celebrate her eighteenth birthday with friends, then she never came home. One of her friends said the last time she'd seen her, the teen had just had an argument with a boy living in Hardin.

When her aunt, Percelia Buffalo Bulltail, went into town to report her missing, the response from law enforcement was the same as always. The officer she spoke to didn't seem to take her seriously, wouldn't give her any forms to fill out, didn't print out any posters, and just jotted down some vague information on a tablet he kept in his pocket.

On August 29, news rippled through Hardin—the body of a young girl had just been discovered. Kaysera's aunt rushed to the sheriff's office for more information, but was given no clear answers.

Every day for fourteen days, the girl's loved ones drove the one hundred ten miles from their home on the Crow Reservation to the Hardin County Sheriff's Office. And every time, they were met with closed doors. Until September 11, 2019, when the other shoe dropped: Jane Doe was, in fact, Kaysera Stops Pretty Places. It had taken almost two weeks to get the family this confirmation. And their ordeal was far from over.

The coroner, who had also performed the autopsy on Henny Scott eight months earlier, stated that decomposition changes in the remains made it too difficult to determine the precise cause of death. The authorities weren't ruling out foul play, but they weren't ruling out an accident either. They suggested Kaysera had simply walked over into someone's backyard, lain down, and died. The family pointed out contradictions in the investigation. How could it be that in the middle of summer, no one had noticed a decomposing body in a yard that was in plain sight of a busy street in a suburban neighborhood?

Kaysera's remains were transferred to the Big Horn County coroner who, in addition to being the local coroner, was the owner of a funeral home. He swiftly cremated Kaysera's body, which her family claims was done against their wishes. For her loved ones, this was "another slap in the face" because, according to Crow spirituality, the dead can neither rest nor move on to the next life if they are cremated.

Again, her family raised a critical issue. A few weeks earlier, Kaysera had filmed and posted the beating of her brother by Big Horn County deputies. Now her relatives were hearing one of the deputies was involved in the investigation into her death. Kaysera's loved ones were sure county law enforcement was trying to hide something or protect someone.

In the months that followed, people held gatherings and rallies, demanding that justice be served. Henny Scott's mother, Paula, walked alongside them, pressing the authorities for answers or, at the very least, a proper investigation.

It is unclear if Selena Not Afraid knew Kaysera Stops Pretty Places personally. But in a gesture of solidarity, the Crow teen joined one of the walks held in her name. Four months after Kaysera's death, Selena also went missing.

On January 1, 2020, after a New Year's Eve party in Billings, the sixteen-year-old hit the road with a few buddies, heading home to Hardin. They were driving along Interstate 90 when their van broke down, so they pulled into a rest stop to troubleshoot the problem. Their stories about what happened next don't all line up, but one thing is for sure. Once the van was running again, the group took off without Selena, leaving her alone at a deserted rest area fifty miles from home, along the country's longest interstate highway, which thousands of truckers drove every day. Selena Not Afraid never made it home.

On both the Crow and Cheyenne reservations, news got around, and just as with previous searches, volunteers gathered where the missing teen was last seen. Cars, trucks, and horse trailers crowded into the rest area. People unpacked stoves, handed around walkie-talkies, and built fires, while volunteers fanned out across the surrounding area, wasting no time. The sad truth was they were getting the hang of it.

Within just a few hours, the rest area was transformed into a bustling command post. Cary Lance, aka White Buffalo, was there, along with Theresa Small, the Cheyenne rescue coordinator. In the cold dead of night, RVs provided warmth and light, and volunteers were fed hot meals. Photos of Selena Not Afraid were printed, while her family flooded social media with appeals for help in finding her.

At the same time, her loved ones notified the authorities, though they didn't expect much of a response. They were surprised when a cavalcade of law enforcement officers and agents rolled in to join the volunteer search team. As far back as Crow and Cheyenne tribal members could recall, this scale of police resources had never been deployed to search for a missing Native girl.

Together, people from the Big Horn County Sheriff's Office and the BIA set up a search grid. Police officers from South Dakota and Wyoming were sent in to support the search efforts. Thermal drones were flown over the area, and eventually helicopters were sent out as well. The local community held its breath.

Luella Brien, a Crow journalist, wrote that Selena Not Afraid might actually have a chance of being found quickly. But her hopes were short-lived. Search efforts dragged on for three long weeks, during which the rest area was perpetually busy.

Selena's mother camped out in the parking lot and slept in her car, waking up only to turn on the engine for warmth. She stared out, glassy-eyed, over the vast frosty landscape. Over time, the search headquarters became a place for prayer, where candlelight vigils were held. Another missing girl? Again? Every time was one girl too many.

When the news finally broke, resentment simmered in the community: Selena Not Afraid had been found dead, her body frozen in a field less than a mile from the highway. In the wake of this discovery, a reporter from the *New York Times* came to town. The national press? That, too, was unexpected. The headline read, "Rural Montana Had Already Lost Too Many Native Women. Then Selena Disappeared." The article explained that families were "raising alarms through social media and even bracing themselves against Montana blizzards to keep their loved ones from being forgotten."

The stories of Henny, Kaysera, and Selena are quite similar. In their short lives, the three Native teens experienced the brutal reality of reservation life firsthand. Henny Scott had lost her brother to suicide. Growing up, Kaysera Stops Pretty Places had been bounced around from one home to another, at times neglected by alcoholic parents, before she was taken in by her grandmother and aunts. Selena Not Afraid had lost one relative after another. There was her brother, killed in a police shooting; then one of her sisters died in a hit-and-run; and her twin sister committed suicide when they were eleven. Extreme violence and indifference plagued both the lives and deaths of these girls in the same way.

But something had changed between Henny's disappearance in 2018 and Selena's in 2020. The families were no longer willing to stay silent. And the media was listening. Things finally seemed to be changing. So, when the autopsy report came out, stating that Selena Not Afraid had died of hypothermia, people were irate.

On the two reservations, the deaths of the three young girls have come to be described in this way: "If Henny was the spark, and Kaysera was the kindling, then Selena was the forest fire that just ignited across the media."

As Crow journalist Luella Brien explains, people began to wonder, "What the hell is going on in this community that allows it to be so easy to disappear . . . over and over and over. Girl's missing for two weeks. Girl's missing for five days. Girl's missing for seven days. Girl gets found. Unexplained injuries. Unexplained disappearance. Hypothermia. Undetermined. Every single time. Really, what the fuck is going on?"

3.

# MISSING AND MURDERED INDIGENOUS WOMEN

Some of Annita Hetoevehotohke'e Lucchesi's ancestors are from Italy. The other side of her family is from the place where the Ho'honáéva, or Rocky Mountains, meet the tóhtoo'éšé'e, the Cheyenne word for "plains." Annita herself, a woman with a broad face and bright eyes, grew up far from these lands, in Louisiana. Over the years, she moved several times, from one end of North America to the other, eventually settling down in the wide-open spaces of southeastern Montana, where she lives with her dogs and horses. She chose to make her home and carry out her mission on her ancestors' territory, not far from Lame Deer.

Her project, which eventually became her life's work, began in 2016. At the time, she was a cartographer and a doctoral student at the University of Lethbridge, in Alberta, Canada, where she was trying to find data about missing and murdered Indigenous women on both sides of the border for a mapping project. But she had a problem: Canadian datasets were incomplete and US data were practically nonexistent.

One evening, at her kitchen table, she started compiling information herself, using press clippings and statements pulled from social media to fill in a spreadsheet. The stories she read were unbearable—about women who were stabbed, doused with gasoline and burned alive, left to die in ditches, found in riverbeds or under trailer homes, or just up and vanished without a trace. After only a few months, she already had a list of a thousand names.

This led her to collaborate with the Urban Indian Health Institute to conduct a study on the same topic. It was a massive undertaking, with researchers recording 5,716 cases of missing and murdered Indigenous women in the United States for the year 2016 alone. In comparison, the Department of Justice database listed only 116 cases. Looking back, Annita says she was "naive" at the time, thinking the project would have an end date.

But she never stopped counting, listing, and cataloging names.

Eventually, this led her to create the Sovereign Bodies Institute (SBI), an independent national database. Working with a team, she attempted to cover the entire country and interview as many families as she could, on the ground, gathering people's stories, cross-referencing sources, and collecting the names of all the Native American women who had been murdered or been reported missing without ever showing up on law enforcement radar.

The grief she witnessed when engaging with the victims' relatives was overwhelming and drove her to fundraise in order to help families access services such as financial assistance, legal aid, and counseling. Resources were limited, and she often ended up addressing each situation herself, one at a time. Annita's phone was always on, and it wasn't unusual for it to ring late at night.

In those days, she wasn't the only person tallying names. Many Native American researchers, women like her, were also digging up stories about women who had vanished and compiling statistics. They all knew no one would believe them unless they published precise, accurate data. So they undertook study after study, each more chilling than the last.

On some reservations, Native American women were ten times more likely to be murdered than the average American. At least 90 percent of Native American women had experienced violence in their lives. In the United States, one Native woman went missing every eight hours. And one in four missing and murdered Native females were minors at the time of their disappearance. Some of these murders were particularly violent, with victims found dismembered or burned. In the land of the free, Native American women were statistically more likely to be raped or murdered than to attend university. And no one cared.

Worse yet was the fact that the datasets were incomplete, meaning the reality was likely much more egregious. Sometimes no one even noticed when a woman went missing. Those who vanished tended to be vulnerable young girls who'd had a falling out with their families or who'd been put into foster care. Some families refused to tell their story because they couldn't trust this system that had betrayed them time and time again. Others kept quiet for spiritual reasons. According to Crow beliefs, for instance, it is disrespectful to talk about the deceased long after their death, as this can disturb their spirit. Thus, dozens of cold cases were being forgotten, forever.

In Canada, the same crisis had been widely recognized for years, with victims referred to as Missing and Murdered Indigenous Women, or MMIW. There was a hashtag for the movement too, #MMIW, and a symbol—a red handprint painted over a person's face and mouth, brought to the mainstream in 2019 by a Native American runner in the Boston Marathon.

In her spreadsheet, Annita sorted MMIW cases by state and county. The issue plagued all Native territories, but two places in the US appeared to be especially dangerous for Indigenous women. One was in Northern California, the other in southeastern Montana, where Henny, Kaysera, and Selena were found dead. Annita now lives in that same county, where she says, "Our cemetery is nothing but a mass grave, with no justice and no interest in seeking it out."

The two counties have a few things in common: endemic poverty, unresponsive law enforcement, and vast, remote reservations set in the heart of an inhospitable wilderness. It's hard to control what goes on in these lawless places, where people live in the forgotten corners of a society that has consigned them to oblivion.

Northern California, the epicenter of cannabis production in the United States, is a hotbed for trafficking of all kinds. Deep in misty forests, people go missing all the time. In Montana, the weather is just as hostile, and life is equally remote. In this part of the country, Native women make up just 3 percent of the population, but they account for 30 percent of missing person cases. Montana is the epicenter of a national crisis.

And while Ashley Loring HeavyRunner, Henny Scott, Kaysera Stops Pretty Places, and Selena Not Afraid became the faces of the cause, there are so many more cases; between 2001 and 2019 alone, two hundred Native American women were killed in Montana. That's nearly one per month.

For a long time, the authorities downplayed the figures published by researchers, citing the lack of access to these independent databases. In fact, the Montana Department of Justice was proudly reporting that it had solved 97 to 99 percent of missing person cases, which tended to involve female teenage runaways who were located soon after they were reported missing. But to anyone who spent any time on one of the reservations, it was clear that, as always, there were two sides to the story. The reality painted by law enforcement and government authorities simply did not line up with the lived experience of Native American families.

In the communities that were hit the hardest by the crisis, among the Blackfeet, the Crow, and the Northern Cheyenne, or among the Yurok, the Hupa, and the

Round Valley tribes in Northern California, everyone knew at least one missing or murdered girl or woman. In a White community in the United States, these kinds of statistics would be unfathomable.

It was the same story every time. A woman goes missing. The authorities, underfunded or uninterested, reply that she's probably out partying somewhere. Her family goes looking for her. Some never end up finding their missing loved one. Some find a body. The investigation is quickly closed or left open until it is forgotten. The families never get answers.

Then another report published in 2019 suggested that half of investigation findings following the death of a Native American woman in Montana were erroneous. Suicide, overdose, and hypothermia were always easier answers, allowing the authorities to quickly move on and skew the statistics. Women were being slaughtered one after another, and no one seemed to be noticing. Each new disappearance awakened a traumatic memory and the same pain, echoing from one end of Montana to the other.

A few months before Selena Not Afraid went missing and not long after Kaysera Stops Pretty Places had vanished, the convoy gathered in Billings at 9:00 P.M. A blizzard warning was in effect, unusual in October, but that didn't deter them. In the dark night, they drove deserted roads in one long line. Among them were several Crow and Cheyenne women, including Theresa Small, who had coordinated the search for Henny Scott. They were headed for Browning, nearly four hundred miles away, traveling across the state in the middle of the night and braving inclement weather to attend an exceptional event. On October 4 and 5, 2019, the Blackfeet Nation would be holding a Missing and Murdered Indigenous Women Tribunal.

It was the first of its kind in the entire country. With the press and cameras present, survivors of violence and families of victims told their stories. They wore red in support of the movement.

It had been two years since Ashley Loring HeavyRunner went missing, and she had yet to be found. So ten months after testifying before the Senate, Kimberly shared her experience once again. With a heavy heart, she spoke into the microphone: "I even feel guilty coming here talking because I should be in those mountains right now searching. But I am my sister's voice now. She deserves to be found, and she deserves justice. She deserves to come home. We were supposed to go explore the world together, but instead I'm exploring the woods for my sister."

For those searching for a missing loved one, time does nothing to ease the pain—it only makes it worse. But that day, Kimberly Loring HeavyRunner found comfort in the company of other victims' relatives and the women pioneering the MMIW movement.

Montana had a problem. Montana was the epicenter of a national crisis. But perhaps it was also the epicenter of a solution to the crisis. The two-day event ended with a march down the streets of Browning. Under a banner bearing photos of Ashley and other missing girls, women from several reservations marched together. It was freezing cold out, and they were just a small group, but they felt united.

After the October 2019 gathering, women from southeastern Montana made several trips out to the Blackfeet Reservation to join search parties. They helped look for Ashley and other missing people. Together, they developed a parallel search system that tapped into word of mouth and the echo of rumors rippling out from one reservation to the next, a process that was sometimes more effective than police interrogations.

In Lame Deer, Montana, people managed to locate a girl in Wyoming using social media. In Browning, residents sent money down to Texas to bring home another girl after an attempted kidnapping. In a hellish circle, the movement was being fed by the very issue it was battling. Each new disappearance brought forth more activists—distraught mothers, sisters, daughters, aunties—who joined the cause, weaving a network from one reservation to the next and spreading across the entire country. They formed a patchwork of interconnected local initiatives without a central organization.

In these communities, some of which had once been matrilineal, women were finding their voice again. And they were no longer willing to stay quiet. "Native American women have always been treated the same. You're silenced. You don't exist," said Theresa Small. "But those years empowered us. We finally have something that belongs to us."

❖

There are so many lingering questions, and just as many outlandish theories, surrounding the deaths of Henny, Kaysera, and Selena. Could the three somehow be related? Several true crime podcasts took the story and ran with it, while documentary film crews made their way to Montana to ask the same question. Invariably, they all pulled at the same thread: Could this be the work of a serial killer? After all, Canada and Alaska both had their fair share of serial killers who'd preyed on Native women. And it was hard to dismiss the theory in this remote part of Montana, where a major interstate highway ran through two reservations.

Initially, Annita Hetoevehotohke'e Lucchesi agreed to discuss the issue in a few interviews, but she eventually stopped trusting the media. It felt like all they wanted were gruesome and sensational details, and she worried that the victims' families would be used as fodder to churn out more true crime content. She also bemoaned the fact that only a few women's names were ever mentioned in the media, while hundreds of women had disappeared in Montana alone, and thousands nationwide.

In every family's quest for justice, a news article or an appearance on TV could make a huge difference. But the system also rendered some victims—the ones who didn't make headlines—invisible all over again. They tended to be older, their stories didn't have enough twists and turns, and they were the most vulnerable ones, the transient ones. And three quarters of missing Native American women never had their first name printed in a newspaper. This was mass femicide.

Instead of looking for real causes, it can be tempting to blame a single culprit. The serial killer is the easy out—the concept aligns with familiar narratives and feeds our morbid curiosity. But reality is far more complex. Annita holds a grudge against certain media outlets, explaining, "The majority of media coverage on this issue frames it like a mystery to be solved when there is no mystery. [. . .] They're fixated on this idea of Native women as rabbits in hats that just kind of magically disappear. And that's not what's happening. We know how and why this is happening, and we know what would fix it."

4.

# AMERICA IS A CRIME SCENE

Officially, she was the first victim in the MMIW crisis. Her name was Amonute, or Matoaka when referred to by her middle name, and she was born around 1595. She was a young Native American living with the Mattaponi tribe in Werowocomoco, in present-day Virginia. Amonute was the favorite daughter of Chief Powhatan, the leader of the Powhatan Chiefdom, an alliance of over thirty Algonquian-speaking tribes.

When a group of Englishmen landed on the nearby Atlantic coast in 1607, they founded a colony called Jamestown. And although the Mattaponi tribe brought the newcomers food to help them survive the cold and famine, tensions eventually flared between the two groups. It is said that Amonute was a skilled interpreter and ambassador, that the teenager fostered relationships between her tribe and the neighboring colony.

At the age of fifteen, the girl was kidnapped and held captive by the colonizers. One year later, she announced her intention to wed an English tobacco farmer named John Rolfe. So she was baptized and renamed Rebecca, which the settlers claimed she did voluntarily. But in the Mattaponi tribe, a different story was passed down through the oral history. It is said that Amonute was raped and that she was pregnant, hence the marriage.

So Lady Rebecca and her husband traveled to England, where this Native American woman in Western dress was presented to the king's court. To some, she was an exotic object, and to others, she symbolized the triumph of civilization. For Amonute, life in exile was unbearable. She died in 1617, when she was in her early twenties, without ever seeing her homeland again, in circumstances that are still debated to this day. Was it illness or poisoning?

Some activists have chosen to use Amonute's name as a symbol, putting it at the very top of the MMIW list—because everyone knows this young Indigenous girl. In fact, she's probably the most famous Native American in the world, though she often goes by her childhood nickname: Pocahontas. However, her actual biography looks more like the MMIW crisis than a love story.

The legend of Pocahontas was distorted from the moment she died, eventually resurfacing in the 1800s, when the country was hungry for national myths. She symbolizes the "good Indian," the one who admired Western culture and religion, the one who preferred to live among Whites rather than alongside her own people. In this version of the story, she represents the original melting pot. Hollywood and Disney took care of watering down the rest. But to some Native American researchers, Mattaponi historians, and activists, Pocahontas's life tells a different story, demonstrating how deep the roots of the MMIW crisis go.

There is evidence of this in a letter sent in 1500, which states, "A great number of merchants go in search of girls; there are at this moment some nine or ten on sale; they fetch a good price, let their age be what it will." The letter is signed by none other than Christopher Columbus. Upon his arrival in the Caribbean, he was already documenting the sexual exploitation of Indigenous girls.

Yet historical research has shown that before European settlers landed on the North American continent, most Indigenous societies honored women, who held spiritual and economic power. In the Blackfeet Tribe, for example, they were "holier than the Pope," says Susan Webber, a professor of philosophy and women's studies at the local Blackfeet University. In many tribes, men who behaved violently toward women found themselves marginalized, barred from positions of power, and even banished. Rape, while not entirely inexistent, was rare. All that changed with the arrival of the first settlers. Like Christopher Columbus, many Europeans described instances of trafficking or widespread sexual violence against Native American women.

As Jodi Byrd, a researcher specializing in Indigenous studies, describes it, "The story of the new world is horror, the story of America a crime." To found "the land of the free," settlers drove populations to starvation, betrayed treaties signed with tribes, and forced people to migrate far from their sacred lands. In the sixteenth century, five to six million Native Americans inhabited what is now the United States. Three hundred years later, only two hundred thirty-seven thousand remained.

In the nineteenth century, they were confined to reservations, deprived of their freedom of movement, stripped of their values and beliefs systems, disconnected from the lands to which they were spiritually bound, and trapped within arbitrary borders. Crow tribal members call this "living within the lines." During this time, and into the 1970s, children were forcibly removed from their families and placed in boarding schools, where they were converted to Christianity and beaten whenever they spoke their language. Widespread cases of physical and sexual abuse in these institutions have been documented.

Once the students aged out, they returned to their families as uprooted adults bearing the burden of their abuse. The trauma was passed down from one generation to the next, perpetuating a cycle of violence, alcoholism, and substance abuse. For five centuries, Native Americans endured systematic extermination, first physical, then economic, and finally cultural. Until recently, they were barely portrayed in pop culture, media, or films, apart from a few stereotypical "cowboy and Indian" roles.

The United States was built upon a mass grave. In his 1963 book *Why We Can't Wait*, Martin Luther King Jr. wrote, "Our nation was born in genocide when it embraced the doctrine that the original American, the Indian, was an inferior race. [. . .] We are perhaps the only nation which tried as a matter of national policy to wipe out its Indigenous population. Moreover, we elevated that tragic experience into a noble crusade." Recently, activists have noted that the fact Native Americans still exist is nothing short of a miracle.

❖

Native American women used to vanish without a sound, leaving their children to grow up with a void, an absence. Living among ghosts seemed normal. For so many years, the crisis was invisible. Stacks upon stacks of cold cases piled up in law enforcement archives, lost in a legal system so complex that even lawyers specializing in tribal law couldn't always agree which agency had jurisdiction over certain criminal cases.

The term "tribal sovereignty" refers to every Native American nation's right to govern itself, form its own government, and control its own territory and its destiny. But the nations were gradually dispossessed of this power through a succession of laws and decrees. The federal government began to crack down in earnest with the Major Crimes Act of 1885, which was passed following the murder of peace chief Spotted Tail, perpetrated on Lakota land. His killer, another Native American man, had been sentenced by the tribe to pay fifty dollars, eight horses, and a blanket as restitution for the murder. Deeming the punishment too lenient, federal authorities intervened and sentenced the man to death by hanging.

This prompted lawmakers to grant judicial authority to federal systems rather than tribes for the most serious of crimes. Native Americans would now have to submit to the White man's law. In 1978, the US Supreme Court decision Oliphant v. Suquamish Indian Tribe effectively created a legal vacuum for all victims of crimes perpetrated by non-Native offenders on Native territory.

In the wake of this ruling, sexual predators, drug manufacturers, and pimps flocked to the reservations, where they knew they were unlikely to be prosecuted for crimes committed on Native land. Their victims were then forced to wander a jurisdictional maze, shuffled between four law enforcement agencies: tribal police, state law enforcement, and two federal agencies—the FBI and BIA.

When a crime occurs in "Indian Country," authorities need to determine whether it happened within the boundaries of the reservation, whether the victim was Native, and whether the perpetrator was Native. The next steps in the investigation will depend on the answers. Each law enforcement organization tends to pass the buck, with no one getting anything done. Investigations fall through the cracks, and some cases are never investigated at all.

With Ashley Loring HeavyRunner's disappearance, as in all missing person cases, the question was even more difficult to answer because it was unclear whether a murder had even been committed. Without an investigation, there can be no justice. Without justice, there will always be more violence. It's a vicious circle perpetuated by systemic problems. At this point, we're no longer dealing with mysterious disappearances; what we are looking at is an erasure reinforced by a society that has chosen to look the other way.

◆

Since she first began her research in 2016, Annita Hetoevehotohke'e Lucchesi has not seen a single conviction—except once for a murder committed at a gas station in front of multiple witnesses. Reservations are lawless lands—they attract outside predators who deliberately target isolated communities, home to the most marginalized people. But in the cases of Henny Scott, Kaysera Stops Pretty Places, and Selena Not Afraid, the families' top suspects are locals. The people they think are responsible for the girls' deaths—or, at the very least, whose negligent behavior led to the deaths—are men they know. They are neighbors, relatives, people the girls trusted when they went out partying.

Some Native men have internalized the racism and sexism directed at Native American women. It took a long time for communities to address this painful issue, which remains a delicate topic. While the men pass on intergenerational trauma and a cycle of violence, the women inherit fear. On reservations, mothers teach their daughters what they should do when they are raped. Not "if" they are raped, but "when" they are raped. The fear lives under their skin, a perpetual knot in their bellies that tightens whenever they leave the house.

Annita Hetoevehotohke'e Lucchesi believes this cycle of violence could end if the tribes regained at least some sovereignty, if they could dispense justice themselves. She knows the system all too well because it once let her down too. There was a time when Annita almost became a statistic herself, added to the long list of missing and murdered women.

5.

# THE ROCKY MOUNTAIN GOAT

The Sovereign Bodies Institute is located in downtown Billings, an-hour-and-a-half's drive from the Northern Cheyenne Reservation. In an overheated building, Annita Hetoevehotohke'e Lucchesi and her teams have set up an office to welcome the families of victims. In the waiting room, there's a small teepee for the children and sage for the spirits. The walls of the meeting room are plastered with a constellation of photos, one for each person who recently went missing or was murdered in Montana. To get an in-person meeting, you have to know one of the employees—no drop-ins allowed. There's no address on the SBI website and no sign outside to advertise their location.

Annita, the SBI founder and director, prefers to keep a low profile and share minimal information about her own whereabouts. Her abuser has been stalking her on social media. It took a long time for her to start opening up about her own story, and she's still relatively guarded, hesitant to go into the details. She's laid out the broad strokes of her story: It happened in Washington State, when an abusive ex forced her into sex work. There was that one day he beat her on the side of the road and all those drivers sped by unfazed. No one stopped, no one intervened. She felt her life was worthless. One of her customers was a police officer who later refused to help her. She went through hell—the violence escalating—and finally, she escaped. And there's this detail: When she first started recording MMIW numbers, all the bones in her left hand were broken, crushed by her ex.

❖

In 2017, when Annita was just one year into her work on the MMIW crisis, the statistics really hit home. For the first time ever, she had to enter the name of someone she knew personally.

During the 2016–2017 school year, she'd been a professor in the humanities and social sciences department at the local Blackfeet Community College, near Browning. One of her students was a young woman just five years younger than her, someone who, like her, was determined to make it out.

That student was Ashley Loring HeavyRunner. She was enrolled in environmental sciences and had signed up for Annita's speech and writing classes. Ashley loved to write. In their end-of-year term papers, Annita had asked her students to imagine how they could best use their degrees to solve a problem in their community. Ashley had chosen to focus on Rocky Mountain goat conservation. But she never finished her project.

The last time Annita saw Ashley was a few months before she went missing. Her student had cried in her arms. She didn't have a truck anymore, and she knew she wouldn't be able to finish the school year without a vehicle. And that was it; Ashley never came to class again.

Every time Annita saw a photo of a Rocky Mountain goat or heard about tribal environmental programs, she thought of Ashley. Adding her name to the list was painful, as it was hard to come to terms with that reality. "That's the bigger ripple effect of this violence that people don't think about, is that when you lose a person, you lose everything they would have accomplished, everything they would have contributed. You know, who will take care of the mountain goats now, because she's not there to do that?"

Around the time Annita had Ashley in her class, many of her students hitchhiked to get around. Some came from Cut Bank, a town on the edge of the reservation, where they hitched rides with truckers on Highway 2 to cover the thirty-five miles to Browning. Annita knew all too well how quickly things could go sideways in these situations. It didn't take much for a Native girl to become an MMIW.

She raised her concerns with the community college president, saying, "Look, one of your students is going to end up trafficked or kidnapped or killed by these truckers." She suggested setting up some kind of school transportation service. But the administration refused flat out, citing a lack of resources.

It took Ashley's disappearance and Kimberly's fight to make locals see the sheer scale of the problem. Shortly after Ashley went missing, another one of Annita's students was found dead in a field in the middle of winter. The official cause of death: hypothermia.

At times, Annita has wondered whether Ashley might have run into trouble while hitchhiking or been dragged into a sex-trafficking ring, because the statistics around sex trafficking are truly chilling. In the US, an estimated 40 percent of sex-trafficking victims are Native American, while Native women constitute only 2 percent of the country's total population. Many people have suggested that Ashley might have been sex trafficked.

One of them is her cousin, Tashina Running Crane, who, in a series of contradictory stories, claimed that her ex, Paul Valenzuela, sold Ashley to a Mexican cartel. Strangely, her theory was corroborated by a police officer who wasn't directly involved in the investigation into Ashley's disappearance. At an event in support of MMIW, he reportedly stated, in front of witnesses, that Ashley had been "sold to Mexican workers."

According to one rumor, she was locked up in a mobile home with several other women, forced to turn ten-dollar tricks and kept high on opiates. Annita dismissed the whole idea as an unlikely lead, a story that "contributes to this widespread misconception around sex trafficking."

For Kimberly Loring HeavyRunner, the idea that a missing girl may have gotten caught up in prostitution is both a meager hope and "the worst feeling there is." She's often wondered about it. "When I imagine that my sister might have been sex trafficked, it's this awful weight, the thought that she could be out there somewhere, trying to get back home."

❖

Sex trafficking and the MMIW crisis are inextricably linked. In Montana, human trafficking cases have risen ninefold since 2015—that's an 871 percent increase—while the number of cartels in the state has exploded. Men from the Sinaloa Cartel, Mexico's most powerful cartel, and the Jalisco New Generation Cartel have been marrying Blackfeet, Crow, and Northern Cheyenne women to get established in the area. They move onto the reservations, seeking new markets and new territories in lawless lands.

In their wake, the number of missing women has also risen. This, in a state that was already grappling with skyrocketing rates of prostitution as transient workers flooded the area during the oil boom. The problem persists to this day, especially along deserted highways deep in Native territory. In fact, at one point, prostitution was so rampant that the Northern Cheyenne Reservation casino banned semitrucks from parking in their lot.

Between Ashley's disappearance in 2017 and the year 2020, as the families of victims became more vocal, several federal initiatives were launched. In an attempt to curb the multiple crises threatening Native American women, the state of Montana and the federal government pumped out one official measure after another.

In 2019, the Trump administration established Operation Lady Justice, a task force dedicated to addressing the MMIW crisis. In 2020, Savanna's Act promised to improve protocols in cases of missing or murdered Indigenous persons. That same year, Congresswoman Deb Haaland, a member of the Laguna Pueblo Tribe, established the Not Invisible Act Commission to develop recommendations in collaboration with survivors and the families of victims.

Annita Hetoevehotohke'e Lucchesi was invited to serve on the commission's panel. And in a speech before Congress, Deb Haaland stated, "Every person deserves to feel safe in their community [. . .] but a long history of violence against Native people has led to the disproportionate disappearance and murder of Indigenous women, girls, and two-spirit people." She called for action, "to finally stop our sisters, daughters, neighbors, and friends from going missing without a trace." Congresswoman

Haaland made this statement just before she was officially named Secretary of the Interior under the Biden administration, making her the first Native American woman to serve as a cabinet secretary.

Things are improving, but Annita Hetoevehotohke'e Lucchesi wonders if it's all just tokenism, people acting like they care without making any real change. It's hard to come up with blanket solutions that will work for all five hundred seventy-four tribes, not to mention all the tribal members living outside the country's three hundred twenty-six official reservations, often under the radar. On the ground, every activist has the same thing to say: The government initiatives have had little effect. Protocols are still vague, with only limited funds allocated to the crisis. The only thing that has truly changed is the growing solidarity between these women.

Together, they are supporting each other as they try to cope with the void left behind by their loved ones. Because every time a woman goes missing, her disappearance has repercussions: Grandmothers have to raise grandchildren on their own, aunts have to take on a second or third job to make ends meet.

Typically, these stories go one of two ways. Either the victim's loved ones fall apart—from what Annita has seen, they often die in the years following the disappearance. She's seen depression, suicide, autoimmune disease, and cancer. Or, in the alternative outcome, the families are driven by their pursuit of justice. Those who survive become fighters, first on behalf of their missing loved ones, then on behalf of the cause. Their rage sustains them, and it feeds on every encounter with a potential suspect—at the local gas station or at the grocery store—until the day that anger morphs into a need for revenge. A tipping point.

# PART 3
# VENGEANCE
# (2020–2024)

## 1.

# THE DOG TAKING GUN'S LEAD

Kimberly Loring HeavyRunner has described it as "the world's worst waiting room." The long hours, days, and nights that turn into months, and then years, all spent waiting for that one phone call, from Ashley or from the police. The call that would bring the closure she'd been wanting for so long.

Ashley had been missing for two and a half years, and her sister had never stopped looking for her. She'd followed every possible lead and played out every possible scenario in her mind. Could Ashley have disappeared on purpose? Maybe she was high and had gone out into the woods, then lost her way? Maybe she'd had a bad encounter—with a human? With an animal? Was she alive? Or dead?

Between 2017 and 2020, Kimberly watched awareness grow, saw initiatives launched and then forgotten, and heard politicians describe a "national crisis." At the end of the day, it didn't change anything for her. Day in, day out, her one and only concern was to find her sister, and she still had no clue where she might be. The call never came. Like many of the victims' friends and family, Kimberly felt abandoned.

On January 18, 2020, she got more bad news. Her father, who had been seriously ill for several years, had died at the age of forty-eight. Roy Lee HeavyRunner left this world without ever finding out what happened to his daughter. The funeral was held ten days later at Little Flower Catholic Church in Browning.

The moment it was over, the whispers and speculation resumed among the small crowd gathered to pay their respects. Since Ashley's disappearance, the rumors had never fully died out. Three names kept coming up. There was Sam McDonald, the man who'd left the last party with Ashley; there was Tashina Running Crane, Ashley's cousin; and then there was Paul Valenzuela, Tashina's partner and Ashley's lover.

During the burial, somebody gave Kimberly a new tip, whispering "Big Al knows something." Big Al, or Alvin Dog Taking Gun, was the owner of the house where Ashley was last seen on the night of June 6 to 7, 2017, before she went off with Sam McDonald. So Kimberly started looking into this umpteenth new lead, though—as she would soon find out—she was already too late.

❖

A month and a half later, on March 3, 2020, the local police got a tip. In a clearing on the reservation, something suspicious had been spotted in a pile of trash. Among the debris, under sheets of plywood, officers found a body—or at least what remained of it, as the head and hands had been removed. Since the body could not be identified, it became yet another John Doe.

A week later, on March 10, someone contacted the Blackfeet tribal police again. This time, twenty-nine-year-old Jason Mattson claimed he knew who the dead man was: Alvin Dog Taking Gun. Jason also confessed to the murder, and although he initially agreed to turn himself in, he called the police again as they were driving over to his home. The 9-1-1 dispatcher could hear a woman crying in the background, begging Jason to let her go, while he threatened her with a knife and a gun. She was a family member.

Over the phone, the dispatcher tried to talk him down, asking, "You don't want to hurt a family member, do you?"

Jason replied, "Yes, I do. I like to kill."

The harrowing standoff and negotiations lasted four hours, until the victim managed to escape. Jason was arrested for murder and kidnapping. Big Al's head was never found.

At this point, Jason had already spent years in prison for crimes committed in 2013, when he was twenty-two. It happened one afternoon, after he and a few friends decided to buy some booze, then go drinking and swimming by a river near Glacier National Park. At one point, two girls in the group began to argue about a bottle of liquor that had been dropped. When one of the boys tried to break up the fight, the situation escalated.

Jason went back to his vehicle, pulled out a pistol, and fired a shot at him, the bullet whizzing past the boy's ear. As the boy and one of the girls fled into the woods, Jason kept on shooting at them, emptying his pistol. The boy was injured in the altercation, with one bullet just missing his spine, but he fully recovered, and the case went to court. The girl who had run into the woods with him acted as a witness. Her name? Ashley

Loring HeavyRunner. Jason was sentenced to four years in prison.

When Kimberly found out about all this in early 2020, she tried to connect the dots. So Big Al had known something about Ashley, but then he was beheaded by Jason Mattson before he could tell her family anything about it. Or maybe Jason knew Ashley and had a motive to hurt her? Kimberly couldn't stop thinking about it, but a lot of folks around town didn't buy the story. They said Jason's brutal attack on Big Al likely had more to do with a shady meth deal. Plus, Jason had still been in prison when Ashley went missing in June 2017. Unless he had an accomplice on the outside, he couldn't have made her disappear. But to Ashley's family and friends, the whole thing was baffling. What had Big Al really known? The family figured he'd taken a piece of the puzzle with him to the grave.

And he's not the only person to have met such a violent end. According to Kimberly, in the years following Ashley's disappearance, four people in the same circle, people who "potentially knew something," all died. Death by decapitation. Death by car accident. Death by gunshot. Was it just a coincidence, or were witnesses being taken out? Kimberly could understand if people knew something and were too scared to talk, because the suspects operated in a world of violence. And Big Al's death had driven that point home.

❖

"Good day. I don't have time to waste, but I know where Ashley is. Contact me as soon as possible. I would like to speak to the family only. I know where Ashley is. She's alive."

The message was sent to Kimberly on Facebook in February 2020 from an anonymous account.

Kimberly wrote back: "Where is she? How do you know this?"

"Calm down, she's been with my uncle, in my basement."

"I am calm."

"She's been going through a lot, but she's fine."

They messaged some more, and Kimberly asked for proof, for any reason she should believe him. The caller was asking for $10,000 in exchange for information about Ashley's whereabouts. Kimberly didn't take the bait. She'd gotten so many of these cryptic messages from people trying to gain something from her desperation. Some of her own contacts thought they had information. Others got in touch anonymously, making ransom demands. A few psychics talked about what they'd seen in visions, and one claimed they'd seen Ashley tied up in a cellar with other women. Every false lead compounded her trauma and made her feel more discouraged.

After two and a half years of searching, Kimberly felt utter despair. Her investigation was stagnating, and the few potential witnesses she could talk to had disappeared one after the other. Her family gradually stopped talking about Ashley in the present tense. In a last-ditch effort, Kimberly sent out pleas to journalists. Then one day in 2020, she received a different kind of message. Her cries for help had been heard, and a second investigation was about to begin.

# 2.
# VIGILANTES

It all started with a Netflix show. When *Making a Murderer* came out in 2015, twenty-eight-year-old Payne Lindsey dove headlong into the hard-hitting documentary, which explores the failings in the American justice system. A director himself, Payne was blown away by the show and decided he wanted to produce an investigation of the same caliber. So he did a quick Google search for the terms "cold case in Georgia," found a case in his home state, invested in a microphone and—without any experience in journalism—chose to investigate the mysterious disappearance of a former beauty queen who'd gone missing in 2005.

After eight months of hard work and dedication, he released his first true crime podcast. It was an instant success. His career took off a few months later when the Georgia Bureau of Investigation announced two arrests in connection with the case and officially thanked Payne for his work. *Rolling Stone* devoted an entire article to the "podcast [that] helped solve a cold case."

Payne Lindsey had found his calling. He felt pulled toward unsolved cases that had somehow slipped under the radar of the mainstream media, with families left to fend for themselves in rural, remote areas where justice was hard to come by. Faced with an inequitable legal system, the loved ones of missing persons sometimes turned to true crime podcasters and internet sleuths to fill in the gaps. With each new season, countless messages poured into Payne's inbox from people asking for help. As he communicated with the relatives of missing people, he started to notice a pattern, a reality that could no longer be kept quiet: the MMIW crisis. How could anyone ignore it, when hundreds of testimonies were flooding in from the families of girls who had vanished?

In 2020, when Payne got a message from Kimberly, he didn't need to give it much thought. The case so clearly epitomized the crisis. So Payne made his way to Browning, Montana, to meet Ashley's sister for the first time. It was the start of a long quest for answers.

With Kimberly's help, Payne went over the most troubling points of the investigation, one by one, before heading out to interview the people involved in the case. His first stop was Sam McDonald's cabin on Saint Mary Lake. He kept his microphone running as he drove down the secluded dirt road. He was used to showing up on people's doorsteps, but you could hear the fear in his voice when he said he was "scared as hell."

No one had told Sam that Payne was coming by, yet when he rolled in, it was as though the man had been expecting him. Sam was leaning against one of his cars in a strange position, his arm fully extended inside the passenger side of the vehicle. As Payne and his colleague stepped closer, Sam pulled his arm out and pointed a gun at them. He greeted them with "I got fucking cameras, I was watching you guys," then relaxed when he learned what the journalists were up to, adding with a chuckle, "If I'd seen a gun out in your hand, I would've shot your ass." He agreed to give an interview but kept his gun within reach. It sat on the table for the entire conversation.

Despite the rough start, Sam was cooperative and seemed to feel bad about how things had gone with Ashley. He was fifty years old, the last person to have seen her, and he said her disappearance had been like a shock to his system. He told them about a dream he'd had in which he'd seen Ashley again, just a few months after that terrible summer. Apparently, she'd told him to turn to Jesus, so Sam complied, leaving behind a "five-year bender," and a meth addiction. "I abused my first two wives. I was a mean man when I was younger. It's just the way you get raised. My stepdad beat my mom. It's a curse. You gotta stop it." But he says he never would have hurt Ashley. "I got nothing to do with her. All I did was party."

Sam has always stuck to the same story. Ashley spent a few days at his place, he eventually dropped her off where Paul Valenzuela was going to pick her up, because she asked him to, and then he fell asleep. In the interview with Payne, he says that Ashley told him she thought she was pregnant. She'd asked him, "Sam, do you believe in women's intuition?" And added, "I think you got me pregnant that first night."

Looking back, Sam figures "If they killed her, they killed my kid too."

But did Ashley really tell Sam about a pregnancy? Or did he find out later through the rumor mill? Apparently, she had, in fact, told her family she was pregnant, but that conversation happened before she went to Sam's. Her relatives think they know who the father is, but they don't want to share his name. They claim he isn't one of the suspects.

In his interview with Sam, Payne asked how he met Ashley. Sam told him it happened at Big Al's house and added, "He's dead too." "Too." That one little word carried so much weight. What did Sam mean by that? Payne didn't ask about it and later explained his thought process to his listeners. At this point, three years after Ashley had gone missing, few people thought she was still alive. Maybe Sam was just thinking the same thing as everyone else. Still, it was hard not to wonder. Every argument Sam put forward to defend himself always seemed like it could be used against him too. Toward the end of the interview, he teared up and threw out an accusation: "I believe if Ashley was around, she'd still be in my life. Either as a good friend, my wife, or a girlfriend. Tee did something to Ashley." "Tee" is Tashina Running Crane's nickname.

◆

Since 2017, a few changes had turned Tashina's normal life upside down. She became a mother in the spring of 2018, while the father, Paul Valenzuela, was in prison. Apparently, they were on a break again after patching things up a few times. There had also been a few constants in the young mother's life: trading insults with her cousin Kimberly through social media posts and writing confusing responses whenever she tried to defend herself.

When Payne contacted her for an interview, she blew hot and cold, then eventually stood up his team. But they did manage to meet in the end. Sam had accused her, and now she was returning the favor. She claimed Sam's son told her Ashley had "flipped out on Sam," adding, "She's like eighty pounds soaking wet, right? I mean, Sam put his hands on her and choked her with his son there. I wanna go do some fucked-up shit to them but I got a daughter now, I can't."

Tashina had plenty of loose claims, wild theories, and vague, unverifiable rumors to share. She said Paul tried to set her up and described a plot cooked up by Paul, Sam, and even Loxie, Ashley's mother. According to one persistent rumor, they'd apparently "sold Ashley to the Mexicans," and they were trying to pin the blame on Tashina. She, too, ended her interview in tears. "I'm tired of being blamed. My Uncle Roy died thinking I killed his daughter."

Kimberly Loring HeavyRunner had spent three years looking for her sister, and now Payne Lindsey was doing the same, navigating murky waters and getting lost in the tangled leads of the investigation, tossed between dubious rumors and unreliable witnesses. Sam had cried. Tashina had cried. Was it all just an act? He wondered, why the tears? Both seemed to be at their wit's end, ostracized and hounded by the town gossip.

When Payne Lindsey takes on an investigation, he pulls out all the stops. After interviewing every person involved in the case, he brought in cadaver dogs to eliminate a few hypotheses. They searched the area where Sam said he dropped off Ashley and the property around Tashina and Paul's old trailer, where Tashina had noticed that "dead smell" after coming back from Seattle in June 2017. That was where Kimberly had cut out a piece of carpet with a reddish stain. The dogs didn't come up with anything. But in this windswept landscape, the weather could make things complicated. Search dogs might miss something if the breeze was too strong or when working in sweltering conditions.

Once Payne had methodically explored every lead, he had one person left to interview. And given his reputation, this person was by far the most intimidating. Paul Valenzuela had been released from prison in the fall of 2018, just over a year after his arrest in Washington

State, and was living in a remote area an hour out of Great Falls. Tashina cautioned Payne, saying, "I just need you to be careful when you go there. If he's selling drugs, he'll pull a gun on you. Or he'll release his dogs. He has a new pit bull."

❖

As Payne drove deeper into this remote corner of Montana, surrounded by rocky terrain and dirt roads that follow winding silty rivers, he spotted a trailer. It belonged to Valenzuela's neighbor. The man said he hadn't met the infamous Paul but reiterated Tashina's advice: "Watch out for him."

With the two warnings in mind, Payne cautiously knocked on Paul's door. A young man in his twenties let him in and went to get Paul from the basement. As Payne waited in the kitchen, every second felt like an eternity. Eventually, Paul came up, but he initially seemed to think Payne had been sent by his landlady. The journalist clarified, explaining, "I'm working with Kimberly." A heavy silence filled the room.

"Wow," said Valenzuela. "You gotta go, bro."

Lindsey pushed back. He'd come to hear Valenzuela's side of the story.

"My side of the story is I know nothing, I see nothing, I hear nothing, and I want nothing to do with it." Things became heated, and Paul went off, shouting, "Alright, people fuck with my life and I get pissed off. Anything that I'm telling you right now. If I find out it's written down [. . .] I'm gonna come find you, okay? [. . .] I ain't got nothing to do with that Loring girl. Okay, never did, never will. Kimberly Loring is a piece of crap. For what the fuck she's been doing to my family. Don't bother me. I don't give a fuck where you come from, man."

Payne gave it one last try, explaining that he'd spoken with everyone, to Sam McDonald and Tashina Running Crane. This set Paul off again. "Tee is a fucking piece of crap too, you can write that down," he spat, then went back into the house and slammed the door behind him. From inside, he yelled, "Get the fuck off my porch before I send the dogs out there."

Payne complied, and when he got back to the car, he could see Paul watching him through the basement window. This is the only time a journalist has approached Paul Valenzuela.

On that trip out to Montana, Payne met with Sam McDonald a second time. This time, Sam handed him a journal he'd kept after Ashley's disappearance, as he attempted to piece together all the details.

"Saturday. We took a cruise this morning, and I was drinking Twisted Teas. We cruised and laughed till about 2:30 or 3:00 P.M. that afternoon. We then went back home, and we got in bed and had sex for the second time. I passed out. Around 5:30 P.M., my son woke me up and asked where Ashley was. I said, 'She must be here. She was before I passed out.' I got up and looked for her, but she was gone. I was hungover and didn't know what to think. I drank a couple Twisted Teas.

"Around 12:30 or 1:00 A.M. that night, Ashley came walking back to the house from the road on the north side of the garage. I asked where she was, and she said something like 'over there,' and pointed toward the way she came from. I never did question her because she had been kind of secretive the last few days. She came back inside for a while, and for some reason she jumped out of my bathroom window. I noticed that she was higher than a kite [. . .]. This behavior went on till 6:00 or 7:00 A.M. She was sitting in and out of my vehicles, walking around the yard, talking to herself, pointing. By this time, I was scared for her, meaning I didn't know what she was on."

In the diary, Sam goes on to explain that once Ashley came down from her trip, he dropped her off near Divide Mountain. "I woke with Ashley on my mind. My heart goes out to her family. Especially Kimberly Loring. She is fighting so hard to find her sister. I wish I could help her. [. . .] Ashley, I wish you were here now. You're the only one who wanted a family with me. [. . .] I'm so empty, Ashley."

Next, Sam added yet another confusing detail to the story. He claimed that shortly after Ashley's disappearance, he got a call from Chris Valenzuela, one of Paul's brothers, and said he recorded and transcribed the call:

"Hey, Sam?

"Yeah."

"I don't know you, but I'm an honest man. And I got a conscience."

"Ok."

"I gotta tell you Paul and Tee killed Ashley [. . .] and they're going to try to frame you."

The thing is, Sam didn't have the recording anymore. He said he'd handed it over to the BIA and the FBI. Again, Payne would have to take his word for it. Sam first accused Tashina, and now it was both Tashina and

Paul. Meanwhile, Tashina first accused Sam and his son, then pointed the finger at Sam, Paul, and Ashley's mother. Paul Valenzuela threatened Payne Lindsey and was refusing to talk. Nothing had changed in Browning.

Perhaps this excerpt about Paul, from an interview with Sam, most aptly sums up their endless dance: "It's called confusion. The perpetrator created this confusion. It's a tactic."

Sam McDonald seemed to be perpetually watching his back. When he spoke to Payne Lindsey, he said he was being targeted by "vigilantes." In truth, it wasn't uncommon for community members to take justice into their own hands on reservations. Sometimes street justice prevailed in the face of a failing justice system.

Everyone knew it happened, but the facts were hazy and poorly documented. Sometimes the vigilante was just hired muscle, someone paid to rough people up and teach them a lesson. Sometimes a group of locals would set up a neighborhood watch, as well as their own emergency line. Sometimes someone would go it alone, in an isolated act of revenge.

Cary Lance, or White Buffalo, the man who searched for missing persons on the Crow Reservation, spent a long time patrolling the vast territory at night. He says for a while, all the people who went missing in the community were "bad guys," people suspected of committing crimes. On the Crow Reservation, it seemed someone had decided to settle the score in their own way. Because when justice is never served, you might be tempted to seek it out yourself.

Sam is sure the same kind of stuff happens in the Blackfeet community. He told Payne, "The whole reservation believes these rumors. They say, like, 'Oh, you had four guys up there rape her and murder her,' and I'm like, 'Fuck you guys, holy shit, you guys are fucked up, you believe rumors and shit too.' This town's crazy, I'm scared, I'm alone. All this shit about revenge, it's never going to stop. They might get me in the end."

He recalled how one evening in the summer Ashley went missing, he got home around 2:30 A.M. after having a few drinks at the casino in Browning. There was a pickup truck waiting for him in front of his place. The driver sped off as soon as he arrived, but he could have sworn it was Paul Valenzuela. The incident convinced him that he was one of Paul's potential targets. He figured Paul wanted to kidnap him. "That motherfucker is gonna torture my son in front of me until I sign something saying I did it. That's the only reason they would want me alive. I will die before they do that."

Sam seemed to live in a constant state of paranoia. He spent his days holed up at home, his eyes glued to the video feed from his surveillance cameras. In his interview with Payne, Sam also claimed that federal BIA agents threatened to put him in jail if he conducted his own investigation. He said the same people also told him not to talk to the tribal police "because four of the [Blackfeet officers] were on Valenzuela's payroll." And he was convinced people were trying to frame him, planting evidence around his home.

Payne sorted through this tangle of paranoid hunches, pulling at the threads, but each one revealed more questions than answers. This had to be one of the most confusing cases he'd ever investigated.

One year of investigations. Twelve episodes. Seven hours of interviews. In 2021, the third season of Payne Lindsey's hit podcast, *Up and Vanished*, was released. It was entirely devoted to the disappearance of Ashley Loring HeavyRunner and reached twenty million listeners. When it first came out, Payne pledged to add another $35,000 to the $15,000 reward already offered by the BIA and the Tribal Council. Now, anyone with solid information about Ashley Loring HeavyRunner would be able to collect $50,000. Four years after Ashley went missing, he was hoping this could jump-start the investigation.

It's hard to know exactly which threats Sam was worried about around the time the podcast was made, between 2020 and 2021. But he was right to feel threatened. Someone was watching him from the shadows. Someone out there did want to hurt him. But it wasn't one of his sworn enemies, Tashina Running Crane and Paul Valenzuela.

3.

# TWISTED TEA

For years, Loxie Loring carried the oppressive weight of her secrets alone. In the past she'd been a drug addict—it was a long desert crossing, a period spent drinking and doing meth. Looking back on that time in her life, she has bitter regrets, but one decision haunts her more than the rest. If it hadn't been for her, Ashley might never have crossed paths with Paul Valenzuela.

One month before her daughter went missing, Loxie went over to the home of an acquaintance, a guy named Clay F., to smoke some weed. Her daughter was with her that day. They hung out in a trailer just a hundred or so yards away from Paul and Tashina's place, on the same plot of land. Since Paul was around, he stopped in to say hi. The man's reputation preceded him, and it made Loxie nervous, so she told Ashley to keep him at arm's length. But her daughter ignored the advice and took off with Paul to do some shooting practice and go for a drive.

When Paul came by the ranch to see Ashley a week later, Loxie told him off—to little avail. Paul and Ashley started seeing each other anyway. And Loxie always blamed herself for bringing her daughter anywhere near that man, and for moving back to Browning in 2011.

When Ashley disappeared, Loxie initially stayed back, dazed by guilt and drugs. On days when she felt up to it, she'd go out looking for Ashley alone, around the spot where Sam said he'd dropped her off. Some evenings, she'd park outside his place to keep an eye on him. His silence, his drinking, the girls who went in and out of his cabin, it all put Loxie on edge. He seemed so unaffected by what had happened.

One day in the summer of 2017, Loxie got her hands on a gun. It was a 9mm pistol that she stashed in the glove compartment before driving out to Sam's cabin by the lake. Her plan wasn't to threaten or scare him. No, she was determined to end his life.

Parked in front of his house in her usual post, she waited for him to return, ready to pull the trigger. But then, at the last minute, she changed her mind. "It's not that easy to kill someone," she explains. "I don't know how they do it, the killers."

How do you find peace when your daughter is missing? When the suspects live in your community? How do you find justice when it is withheld from you? Paul seemed inaccessible, a ghost coming and going. Tashina Running Crane had moved somewhere a few hours away. Loxie used social media to keep track of their lives from a distance. But Sam . . . Sam was always there, so close, on the reservation. Days passed and she quietly brooded, until that one time she could have killed him.

It was a few years ago. She'd been dragged down into a downward spiral of guilt, then drugs to numb the pain, with a growing desire for revenge, which called for even more drugs. Loxie was falling apart. She kept driving to and from Sam's place, parking out front and calling out to him when he was nearby. She lashed out at him, sparking heated arguments. Then one day in 2021, more than three years after Ashley went missing, one of their altercations escalated. Sitting in the driver's seat, Loxie stepped on the gas and drove straight for Sam.

He came away from the incident without any serious injuries, but Loxie was arrested by the county sheriff's office and spent nearly three months behind bars.

Looking back, she's still angry about it. "When we try to get justice, we end up in prison. But they manage to get away with it."

The incident did have one positive outcome. It made Loxie realize she'd gone too far, blinded by her need for revenge. She'd been neglecting her other kids, especially Kimberly. To prove she was better than the suspects, Loxie got herself into rehab in February 2021. She's been sober ever since. It's her way of honoring Ashley.

That same winter, Kimberly moved a thousand miles away from Browning, to the West Coast. Years spent searching for her sister had left her emotionally and physically worn down. She had sacrificed her wedding plans and her career. Before leaving Montana, Kimberly sorted through her little sister's stuff. She found her acceptance letter from the University of Montana, in Missoula, dated 2017. Ashley had pulled it out so many times that the paper was worn thin, almost tearing along the folds.

And there was the notebook in which she'd written these lines by poet Adrienne Rich: "I know you are reading this poem [. . .] on a gray day of early spring, faint flakes driven across the plains' enormous spaces around you." She'd highlighted the words "faint flakes" and commented, "The word faint reminds me of myself as I disappear like a flake in the snow."

As the investigation dragged on, Kimberly found solace in her faith. She was baptized in a church north of Portland in March 2021. To allow herself to move on, she made one last phone call to each of the main suspects. By then, she almost felt bad about feeding Tashina to the wolves on social media. Because of the rumors, her cousin had been fired and she'd struggled with her mental health. With all three suspects, Kimberly spoke of Jesus, prayer, and redemption.

Her call with Paul Valenzuela was tense. Before hanging up, he ended the conversation with this cryptic statement: "Your god can't take away what my god already blessed me with." But Kimberly was unfazed. She knew her God would bring her an answer and explained, "Jesus knows where my sister is, but the suspects don't know where Jesus is."

She also found a new job at a funeral home and spent her days transporting bodies from their place of death to the morgue. She was done with the investigation. When she passed the torch on to Loxie, she told her mom she didn't want to hear about any of the latest developments. She asked for only one thing: "Let me know when you find her." Loxie promised to uncover the truth.

❖

When Payne Lindsey's podcast about Ashley came out in August 2021, Loxie couldn't bring herself to listen to it. She was too afraid of the brutal truths she might hear. But her therapist, an addiction specialist who had become her friend, recommended listening. Accepting what had happened would be an important step in her healing journey. So she started by reading a transcript prepared by her therapist, who'd removed the most gruesome gossip. Next, she got up the courage to listen to the entire season. In each episode, she learned of more horrible rumors: Ashley had been tied to a tree and left to be devoured by animals; Ashley had been cut up in a chipper; Ashley had been raped by four men.

"I can't imagine how Kimberly went through all this on her own, it's so hard," Loxie reflected. But she stuck with it, went back to the text her friend had provided, and took notes, underlining certain words. Could there be a clue somewhere in those long interviews with suspects, hidden among the conflicting stories? Something Kimberly or Payne might have missed? She analyzed every one of Tashina's expressions—that sob wasn't sincere, there was malice in her laugh. And Sam, how could he have been aware of Ashley's pregnancy? Only her youngest sister had known about it. As far as Loxie was concerned, Sam knew things he shouldn't. What if

Sam had been abusing Ashley, so she'd told him about the pregnancy to stop him from hurting her, to protect her child?

Four years after Ashley went missing, her mother picked up the investigation led by her eldest daughter, one piece at a time. Kimberly had never had time to sort out all the leads and rumors and establish a precise timeline. It was Loxie's turn now, and she was searching for "the missing puzzle piece." She interviewed all their friends and family again and pored over the suspects' social media posts, leaving no stone unturned.

In February 2018, Tashina had gotten a Valentine's Day card from Paul, sent from prison. On November 15, 2018, they'd appeared in a video together with their daughter. Loxie recorded Tashina's every move. Trip to Arizona. Trip to New Mexico. Trip to Idaho. Trip to Washington State. And in Montana, she'd been spotted in Billings, Polson, Whitefish, and Kalispell. Loxie was keeping tabs on her. With her therapist, she verified all her alibis and unraveled her lies. Tashina had always said she was married to Paul, but they couldn't find a certificate to prove it.

Over and over again, Loxie read the excerpt from Sam McDonald's diary too, the one Payne Lindsey had shared with her. One day, while scrolling through

Tashina's TikTok account, something clicked in her head. In several videos, Tashina was holding a can of Twisted Tea, a hard iced tea drink. Loxie started to connect the dots. She was sure she'd never seen Sam with that drink, and she hadn't noticed any Twisted Tea cans the few times he'd let her into his home. And yet, in his diary, he wrote that he drank it several times that terrible week in June 2017.

It didn't prove anything, it might not even be a solid lead, but it was enough to get Loxie thinking about a whole new theory: What if Tashina had dictated the diary entry to Sam? What if Sam and Tashina, who'd constantly been accusing each other, were actually accomplices? Sam claimed he'd dropped Ashley off at Divide Mountain so Paul could pick her up, but what if that was a lie they'd told to throw people off? An attempt to mislead the family? Maybe Ashley's loved ones had spent years searching in the wrong location. Loxie had her doubts, but she also had a powerful ally she could turn to for advice.

After her time in rehab, Loxie wanted to distance herself from the reservation, so she moved to a small industrial town called Shelby, an hour east of Browning. Her home is filled with reminders of her missing daughter. She got Ashley's first name tattooed on her forearm and, on the walls of her apartment, she's hung photos of her at prom and at her graduation ceremony. Those are the moments she wants to remember.

Every morning at dawn, Loxie heads off to her new job in the bakery section of her local grocery store. On Sundays, she goes to Mass, and on Thursday evenings, she leads the Shelby Narcotics Anonymous meetings, which she started. She'd almost forgotten what it was like to live as a functional person.

In Shelby, off the reservation, when a young woman goes missing, law enforcement actually responds. She had a bitter reminder of this reality one time when a non-Native girl was reported missing. Within hours, squad cars were dispatched from Great Falls, a town nearly ninety miles away, to support the local authorities.

Loxie also has a more practical reason for moving to Shelby: Her new place is just a couple of hundred yards away from the local FBI office. While her daughter Kimberly grew to loathe federal agents with every disappointment—in fact, most victims' families don't trust them—Loxie is betting on cooperation with the new agent who took over the case in 2022. He's met with her several times, for hours. She brought him all her documents, compiled in a binder, and he took the time to read through them. And when Loxie thinks she might have new information or has a problem, she doesn't think twice about reaching out.

Like the day her son disappeared. Since the tragic summer of 2017, Ashley's brother had spent his days ruminating in his bedroom, his mental health in tatters. In December 2023, when he ran away from home, the new FBI agent helped Loxie locate her son and bring him back. If anyone could help her solve the mystery, it just might be this guy. So Loxie is turning to the podcast again and picking up her investigation where she left off.

4.

# THE FIFTH SEASON

Vandree OldPerson was crazy about Jimi Hendrix, competitive running events, and true crime podcasts. She was just under twenty when Payne Lindsey launched his podcast, and she ate up every episode. And not without apprehension—she was a Blackfeet woman herself, living in Browning. She'd heard of Ashley Loring HeavyRunner like everyone else, but she had no idea how poorly the investigation had been conducted. Flabbergasted, she once told her mother, "If anything ever happens to me, you have to find out what went on."

Less than two years later, in March 2023, Vandree vanished on the reservation. She'd gone out with friends and never came home. Her mother, Carlene Oldperson, was taken aback. Who should she call? The tribal PD?

The FBI? A friend suggested she reach out to Rhonda Grant-Connelly. There was a time when, if someone went missing in the Blackfeet community, Kimberly Loring HeavyRunner was the go-to person, the one who'd bring in help. After she moved away, Rhonda took over.

She, too, had experienced this kind of tragedy first-hand. It was so common on the reservations. Her own nephew, twenty-one-year-old Matthew Rattlesnake Grant, had vanished from the reservation in a blizzard in December 2016. Without any support from law enforcement, she'd Googled how to coordinate a search party. It took volunteers sixteen days to find Matthew's body in an alley in Browning. The FBI deemed it a murder, but no one was ever arrested. Matthew's mother was devastated and committed suicide soon after his death.

When Ashley went missing the following summer, Rhonda joined the volunteers to help her family. She was also there when Vandree went missing. Since that first Google search, the sixty-year-old mother had figured out the basics. So she helped coordinate a search party, out in the freezing cold of March 2023. Volunteers combed the area where Vandree was last seen, and after three days, they found her phone and purse. Her mother Carlene fell apart—Vandree never went anywhere without them. She felt a kind of "silent scream" in her head.

A little farther away, rescue teams found the young woman's body. Her face was swollen and scratched. In the Blackfeet community, Vandree's story reminded everyone of Ashley's disappearance. Both girls were the same age when they went missing. They'd both been struggling with depression after the sudden death of their grandfather. And then, barely out of their teens, they'd started partying and getting mixed up with men twenty years older than them. When Carlene Oldperson told one of the FBI agents on the case about the people Vandree had been seeing, she says he scoffed and said, "Oh, that goes on all the time up here, doesn't it?"

Soon, the investigation was closed. In the autopsy report, there was no mention of the scratches on the young woman's face. Carlene wishes she'd taken a photo of her daughter's body as evidence. According to official records, Vandree died of hypothermia, with severe alcohol intoxication.

A month and a half later, Rhonda invited Carlene to join a rally demanding justice for all the murdered and missing women and girls on the reservation. In spite of herself, Carlene had just joined the movement.

❖

The friendship that binds Loxie, Carlene, Rhonda, and the others began with a few supportive messages on social media. Over time, these bereaved mothers and aunties had to set aside their grief so many times to look for someone else's child or to attend another funeral that they ended up wanting to channel their collective pain into something concrete.

Rhonda, the group's leader, is an exuberant woman who looks like she walked straight out of a 1980s style guide, with her fringe vest, impressive blowout, and purple-tinted glasses. She's a medical assistant and has her phone with her at all times. She always knows what to say. "Call the police." "Ask for the case number." "Contact the hospital." "Print posters." "Don't forget to provide meals for the volunteers." "Make sure to dress warm, it's cold out there." "Watch out for bears."

After losing her nephew and then her sister-in-law, she spent her time alone at home, ruminating. She knows how easy it is to fall apart. So Rhonda and other victims' relatives founded a nonprofit called Blackfeet MMIP, short for Missing, Murdered Indigenous People. With the Tribal Council's consent, they set up their headquarters in a disused building that was once the town's historical museum.

The indefatigable Rhonda has planned a full slate of activities for the organization. They want to offer self-defense courses, join training sessions on how to run a search—organized by other associations and law enforcement agencies throughout Montana—set up a twenty-four-hour hotline for victims' families, and the list goes on. Thanks to her, the other women are able to keep it together.

Through conversations with her new friends, Carlene Oldperson realized that there was nothing normal about what she was experiencing. As she explains, "We're so overwhelmed by the tragedies that we don't react anymore. Suicide, sexual abuse, physical violence. On the reservations, that's just our daily life. If a team of Western sociologists landed here, they wouldn't believe it."

In the core group, there's also a woman called Wilma Fleury. She's shyer than the others, and crippled by the weight of her grief. She found out about the death of her twenty-two-year-old son Willy Pepion in May 2020, on Mother's Day. He died in a tribal prison cell after fighting with other young people from the reservation. Investigators initially deemed his death a homicide, but the BIA closed the case two years later.

Men are also victims of this cycle of extreme violence. That's why the support group that Rhonda founded for the Blackfeet community is called MMIP rather than MMIW. The broader acronym also includes two-spirit people, a term some Native communities use to encompass gender identities outside the binary. Activists have become divided over the concept of a shift to MMIP, as some want to include missing or murdered Native men in the victim count, while others would prefer to stick to the original focus of the movement so it can remain a fight to end violence against women.

When men are murdered, the story tends to go a different way. Their deaths may be the result of police violence. In the US, Native American men are five times more likely than White men, and three times more likely than African American men, to be killed by the police. Other deaths tend to be related to the settling of scores, alcohol and drug abuse, and parties that get out of hand.

Men are also largely absent from the movement. Women gather to protest, and they organize search parties, support each other, and care for the children of those who go missing. Solidarity is at the heart of their social ties, just as it was in ancestral tribal systems. But the men are rarely there. And when they are, it's usually because they've been dragged along by their wife or sister. They linger on the sidelines. As researcher Annita Hetoevehotohke'e Lucchesi puts it, "Our men are kind of 'lost in the Prairie.' That was my dad's expression. I feel like I'm the maid that cleans up [their] messes. The men in my generation have abandoned us."

Since Ashley went missing, the reservation's list of dead and missing people has grown. Arden Pepion, a three-year-old girl, disappeared in April 2021. She and her uncle were on their way to an outdoor shooting range near a river when he says he lost sight of her. A week later, twenty-six-year-old Leo Wagner was seen walking, injured, along a road near Saint Mary Lake. Then he vanished. Both went missing while Payne Lindsey was on the reservation, conducting interviews.

According to some rumors, there might be a link between Leo Wagner's and Ashley Loring HeavyRunner's cases. It's around this time that Rhonda Grant-Connelly began keeping a list. Now, three years later, in 2024, the list features sixty-two MMIP names. That's sixty-two Blackfeet families waiting for answers or for a conviction.

❖

The meeting lasted just a few minutes, and Rhonda immortalized the moment with a selfie. It was March 26, 2024, on a cold and muddy day between two snowstorms, the kind of day only Montana's fifth season can serve up. That Tuesday, a historic event brought together the entire Blackfeet Nation. Schoolchildren had learned songs in Blackfeet, and community Elders were dressed in their best traditional garb—the entire town of Browning was celebrating.

The tribe had dedicated a full day of ceremonies and festivities to celebrate one of their own, Lily Gladstone, who had made it big. She'd just won a Golden Globe for Best Actress—making her the first Native American woman to take home the prize—and had nearly come home with an Oscar in the same category for her role in *Killers of the Flower Moon*. The Martin Scorsese film was adapted from a book by investigative journalist David Grann that explores a series of unsolved murders committed against the Osage community in the 1920s.

On this day at the end of March, Lily Gladstone was receiving another award that, according to one Blackfeet Elder, was "more important than the Oscars" and one of the highest honors the tribe could bestow upon one of its members: a sacred headdress crafted with eagle feathers. It was all happening in Browning, in the place she had grown up. Rhonda admired Lily for both her talent and her commitment to this cause that was so close to her heart.

In late 2023, at an event put on by *Variety* magazine in Los Angeles, Lily Gladstone honored every Rhonda, Loxie, Kimberly, and Annita in the country—all the Native women who were bringing about change. On stage, with tears in her eyes, she'd summed up the MMIW crisis and its complexity in just a few minutes, saying, "The only people who have any authority to do anything do nothing, and the people who are left to do anything about it are these women here, women who have children in our communities." She ended her speech with a Cheyenne proverb, "A nation is not defeated until the hearts of its women are on the ground." And added, "Ladies, I know that we are far from defeated."

Lily Gladstone has since played other roles in films and TV shows about the MMIW crisis. After decades of neglect and caricature, Hollywood seems to be turning a corner in the way the industry represents Native Americans. The conversation is finally happening. Native women are no longer invisible.

❖

The MMIW crisis can be embodied by one object: the simple binder. Nearly every victim's family has one at home, and they all look the same. They are thick, filled with hundreds of documents, some sorted, some not. They contain printouts of email exchanges with law enforcement; screenshots of suspects' social media posts; a shaky timeline, crossed out and rewritten, the dates underlined with a thin pencil; copies of dozens of letters sent to senators, Oprah Winfrey, and Kamala Harris; and Post-it notes with phone numbers. The phone numbers are generally the same numbers across Montana: Annita Hetoevehotohke'e Lucchesi's number, Rhonda Grant-Connelly's number, and Erica Shelby's number.

Erica is a lawyer specializing in tribal law, and she's sifted through many of these binders, including those put together by women from Blackfeet MMIP. She was impressed by their work, explaining, "They did an excellent job at keeping everything. Once we looked at their files, it was a no-brainer that most of these cases are solved. They know who did it." All that's missing is a trial.

In 2024, Erica took over six of these closed cases, in the hopes of getting them reopened. She plans to organize a fundraiser to start a legal consultancy and invest in state-of-the-art equipment to help the families of missing and murdered women and girls. For example, ground-penetrating radar would allow them to cover a larger area and locate human remains more effectively.

Erica is a part of a new wave of Native American women who, like Annita Hetoevehotohke'e Lucchesi, are using their university studies as an opportunity to speak out and take on roles that previous generations were denied. They are activists, and also sociologists, lawyers, police officers, or forensic specialists, like Haley Omeasoo, a young Blackfeet PhD student who chose to study forensic and molecular anthropology after she went through a traumatic event. Ashley Loring HeavyRunner was her classmate, and the disappearance set Haley on a career path dedicated to ending the MMIW crisis.

She hopes to open her own forensics lab by 2026. The first step would be to convince the authorities to centralize operations and have evidence analyzed in her lab, rather than sending it away to different agencies and running the risk of losing it. Next, she plans to create a database of genetic information that would be shared only with the tribe and not with the federal government. This is in response to the fact that Native Americans tend to distrust the government and have largely resisted the genealogy trend that has swept across North America, refusing to send DNA samples to online sites.

Haley is also working on a DNA extraction method that will not damage bones; according to Native American spiritual beliefs, human bones need to remain intact, as the essence of the deceased is held within them. In the early spring of 2024, she scouted a plot of land in the middle of Browning, where she plans to build what will be the very first Indigenous forensics lab in the United States.

That same week in March 2024, Wilma, Carlene, Rhonda, and Loxie were celebrating big news. The organization had received its very first donation check—for $25,000. They wondered what they would do with so much money. "Find answers," said Rhonda, decisively. To celebrate this first milestone, they planned to go out for fry bread, a classic Native American dish. But first, they brewed themselves a strong cup of coffee, or "cowboy coffee," as they like to call it.

5.

# SACRED EAGLE

Back to the previous summer. On August 14, 2023, the clock had just struck midnight when a special task force cordoned off the intersection of Sixth Avenue and Seventh Street in a suburban neighborhood in Great Falls. Vehicles from the FBI and the Pondera County Sheriff's Office surrounded the area, and, this time, the multiple agencies involved in the case were working together.

Journalists knew law enforcement would never go to such lengths for a small-time crook. This was clearly about a major criminal. In the middle of the night, a local TV crew was dispatched to the scene. An FBI agent's voice boomed through a bullhorn, jolting neighbors from sleep. "FBI! Step out of the house!" Everything was still. Then a second noise, the deafening blast of a flash-bang, finally roused even the heaviest sleepers on the block. There was the impact of a battering ram against a door. A few minutes later, a man was dragged into a van, handcuffed and bound at the waist by a heavy chain.

At the end of the following day, Loxie was parked in front of her TV, surrounded by family, filming the news on her cell. Someone had reached out to tell her the FBI had just arrested Paul Valenzuela. When the suspect appeared on the screen, Loxie was ecstatic. "God works in mysterious ways, but rotten fruit will always fall on its own!"

The list of charges brought against him by federal authorities was long and murky. Several investigations seemed to be overlapping. He was suspected of dealing meth, and he and his son had allegedly been involved in an altercation with a gang. Apparently, the argument had gotten out of hand, and his son had shot and killed a man. Paul Valenzuela was also suspected of assaulting his son-in-law with a baseball bat and threatening an FBI investigator.

Nothing indicated whether Paul had been questioned about Ashley's disappearance, but five days later, the FBI did search the trailer in which he and Tashina had lived in 2017. Again, someone gave Loxie a heads-up, so she rushed over to the scene, where eight FBI vehicles were parked outside the trailer home. From the road, she spent forty-five minutes watching people and K-9 units get to work. They were closing in, she thought to herself. After all, Paul had said in 2018 that he was the only person who could lead them to "the people who did all this to Ashley."

Two months went by and then, one day in the fall of 2023, Loxie got another call. A logger had found human bones on the reservation. The FBI sent out a team from Salt Lake City, and everyone held their breath, just as they had five years earlier, the day after Kimberly's speech before Congress. The wait was as unbearable as it had been five years earlier. The conclusion, just as it had been five years earlier, was yet another disappointment. It wasn't Ashley. The remains were those of a person who'd lived off the reservation.

But Loxie couldn't give up hope. She pulled out her binder and started studying each person's alibi all over again. Next, she, too, contacted lawyer Erica Shelby and Haley Omeasoo, the forensics researcher. Haley told her that when winter was over in the Rockies, she'd coordinate more searches for Ashley and the other missing people, with new protocols. Deep down, Loxie is sure they'll find her daughter any day now. It has to happen. She can't lose hope, can't fall apart again.

It's Easter Monday, 2024, and Loxie Loring is finding it hard to hide her grief. Easter was Ashley's favorite holiday. Although it's been seven years since her daughter went missing, Loxie still hasn't dreamed of her. In the meantime, she keeps an eye out for signs everywhere she goes. After weeks of unexpected snowstorms, the sky has cleared, and the sunlight sparkles on white landscapes that will soon surrender to spring.

With a heavy heart, Loxy hits the road again. She speeds by open fields, ranches, snow-capped mountains, and the odd bison scattered across the landscape. Near Saint Mary Lake, still covered in a sheet of ice, she turns onto a dirt road she could drive with her eyes closed. She parks outside Sam McDonald's place long enough to note his absence and the fact that he's started new work on the place.

Then she's off again, headed for Tashina and Paul's old trailer home. From the road, standing at the gate, she can see the neighbor, Clay F., is home. He's a friend of Paul's, and his place is where Loxie had gone with Ashley, around mid-May 2017, to smoke weed. His dogs come running out toward her, their barks menacing, but she is unfazed. She quiets them with a confident, sharp "Lie down!" Loxie Loring is not about to be scared off by a bunch of rez dogs.

Back in 2023, she stood in this same spot, watching the FBI search the premises, and she seems to have a mental catalog of every detail. Then she spots something that would have escaped a less keen eye; it's a dark shape soaring high above the trailer. An eagle. "There are a lot of eagles here, but we don't see them much," she explains. In Blackfeet culture, eagles are a good omen.

The day the FBI searched the trailer, she saw three of them in this same spot. Softly, Loxie says, "Ashley's with me today. She's sending a message." Her eyes brighten, then well up, and her shoulders slump, as if relieved of a weight too heavy to bear. A black cloud has dissipated. This is the sign she'd been waiting for. "We'll dig it all up if we have to. We'll find her. I know she's out there."

**TO KEEP THE INVESTIGATION GOING,**
**FIND UNPUBLISHED DOCUMENTS HERE:**

# APPENDICES

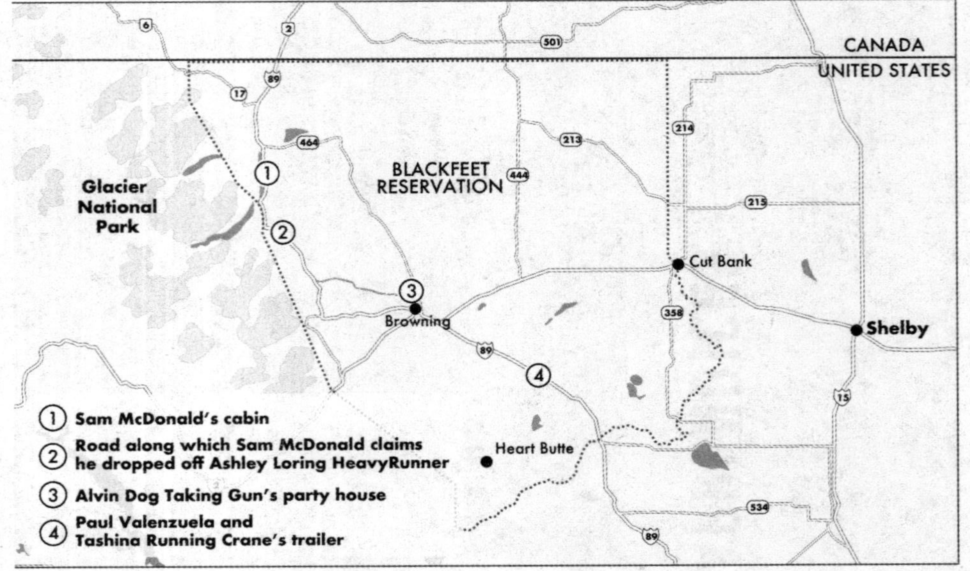


THE BLACKFEET RESERVATION

BLACKFEET RESERVATION
Browning
Great Falls
Helena
Billings
Hardin
Lame Deer
Little Bighorn Battlefield
CROW
RESERVATION
NORTHERN CHEYENNE
RESERVATION
50 km

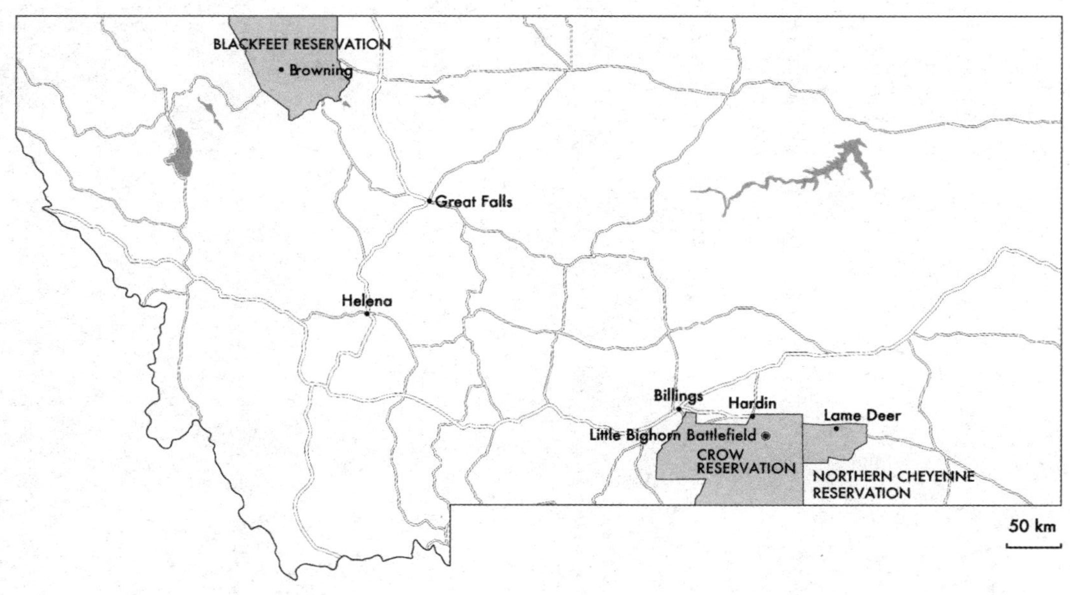

MONTANA

# Glossary

**BIA:** The Bureau of Indian Affairs is the federal agency responsible for implementing US laws and policies related to "American Indian, Native Hawaiian, and Alaska Native peoples." The BIA has its own police force.

**MMIW:** Missing and Murdered Indigenous Women. Some people and organizations also use the term MMIWG, which stands for Missing and Murdered Indigenous Women and Girls.

**MMIP:** Missing and Murdered Indigenous People.

**SBI:** The Sovereign Bodies Institute coordinates research and support for the families of MMIP crisis victims.

# Timeline

**1617:** Amonute, also known as Pocahontas, dies—modern-day activists now call her the first Missing and Murdered Indigenous Woman.

**June 25–26, 1876:** The Battle of the Little Bighorn, or the Battle of Greasy Grass.

**1885:** The Major Crimes Act is passed, granting judicial power to federal authorities rather than tribes in the event of a serious crime.

**March 6, 1978:** The Supreme Court rules that "Indian tribal courts" do not have the authority to try and punish "non-Indians."

**December 17, 1979:** Seven-year-old Monica Still Smoking goes missing on the Blackfeet Reservation. Her body is found soon after her disappearance.

**June 5, 2017:** Ashley Loring HeavyRunner leaves her father's home. This is the last time a family member will see her alive.

**Night of June 5–6, 2017:** House party at Vernon's, where Ashley's friends refuse to give her a ride home.

**Night of June 6–7, 2017:** Ashley is spotted by several witnesses at a house party at the home of Alvin Dog Taking Gun, aka Big Al. One witness says they saw her leave with Sam McDonald in the morning.

**June 8, 2017:** Kimberly Loring HeavyRunner lands at the Missoula airport at 10:25 P.M. That same day, Ashley logs onto Messenger for the last time.

**June 11, 2017:** Sam McDonald allegedly drops Ashley off near Divide Mountain, where she says she is meeting Paul Valenzuela, aka V-Dog.

**Mid-June 2017:** Ashley's family contacts tribal law enforcement to report her missing.

**Late June 2017:** Law enforcement receives reports of a woman resembling Ashley running away from a vehicle along Highway 89. The first search parties go out looking for Ashley.

**November 14, 2017:** Ashley's name is registered in the National Missing and Unidentified Persons System.

**February 2018:** The FBI officially takes over the case.

**December 8, 2018:** Fourteen-year-old Henny Scott goes missing.

**December 12, 2018:** Before Congress, Kimberly tells her story and addresses the lack of resources for law enforcement and judicial services on reservations.

**December 28, 2018:** Henny Scott's body is found. Despite visible injuries on the victim, hypothermia is deemed the most likely cause of death.

**August 29, 2019:** Kaysera Stops Pretty Places is found dead in Hardin, Montana. Law enforcement does not notify the family until fourteen days later.

**October 4–5, 2019:** The Blackfeet Nation holds a tribunal about MMIW cases, a first in the United States.

**January 1, 2020:** Selena Not Afraid is reported missing. Her body is found on January 20. The official cause of death is hypothermia.

**March 3, 2020:** Alvin Dog Taking Gun is murdered. A week later, Jason Mattson confesses to the crime.

**October 2020:** Savanna's Act is passed; it aims to improve protocols and practices in MMIP cases.

**October 2020:** The Not Invisible Act Commission is established so government entities can collaborate directly with survivors or families of victims to develop solutions to the MMIP crisis.

**March 2023:** Vandree OldPerson goes missing and is eventually found dead. According to the autopsy report, the cause of death is hypothermia, with severe alcohol intoxication.

**May 5, 2023:** President Joe Biden officially declares May 5 "MMIP Awareness Day."

**August 14, 2023:** Paul Valenzuela is arrested by the FBI in Great Falls.

# The Blackfeet Nation MMIP List

People who went missing on the reservation:

**Gabriel Calfbossribs** – 2024

**Arden Pepion** – 2021

**Leo Wagner** – 2021

**Ashley Loring HeavyRunner** – 2017

Unsolved deaths on the reservation:

**Jaydie Butterfly** – 2025

**Madison Miller** – 2025

**Corbett Laplant** – 2025

**Anthony Gervais** – 2024

**Vandree OldPerson** – 2023

**Michelle Lynn LazyBoy** – 2023

**Kenneth Lee Bostwick II** – 2023

**Irvin Ingram** – 2022

**Amber Littledog** – 2021

**Tony Little Dog** – 2021

**Willy Wayne Pepion** – 2020

**Brittney Sue Madplume** – 2019

**Michael "Skinny" Campbell** – 2018

**Tony Michell** – 2017

**Zachary Gervais** – 2017

**Matthew Grant** – 2016

**Charles Daune Devereaux** – 2015

**Alexandria Home Gun** – 2014

**Darryl Morris** – 2014

**Patricia Little Young Man** – 2013

**Carol Trombley-Salway** – 2013

**Ken Kelly Rattler** – 2013

**Tanau Thomas** – 2012

**Eugene Stevens** – 2011

**Kello James Kipp** – 2008

**Israel Shorting** – 2008

**Bill Whitequills** – 2007

**William "Billy" Matt** – 2007

**Thomas Gordon Powell** – 2004

**John Thomas Small** – 2003

**Marty Standing Rock** – 2002

**Josie Salois-Running Wolf** – 1998

**Patricia Duckhead Buehl** – 1993

**Gordon Takesgun** – 1992

**Monica Still Smoking** – 1979

**Luella "Cookie" Vielle**

**Mabel Weaselhead-Calfrobe**

**Charmaine Pepion**

**Marie GreenNeckless-Runningwolf**

**Marlene Boy**

**Jaqueline Desiree Pepion**

**Stella Calftail-Vielle**

**Gail Robin Sharp**

**Mary Anne Running Crane**

**Aaron North Piegan**

**Wade Zane Gobert-Laplant**

**William "Billy" Edwards**

**Levi Many Hides**

**Allen Spencer**

**Anthony Arrowtopknot**

**Charlie "Ronald" Calfrobe**

**Danny Daniels**

People who went missing or were killed off the reservation:

**Sukaki Many Hides**

**Whisper Sellars**

**Kimberly Lynn Gobert**

**Misty Upham**

**Danett Calfbossribs**

**Leonard Kieth Eagle**

**Judy Ann Gallagher Hanway**

**Jamie Takes Gun**

**Mika Westwolf**

**Garnet Ann Bear Child**

**Clarence "Rosco" Running Wolf Moon**

**Norma Madeira**

List compiled by Rhonda Grant-Connelly and updated in July 2024. Some dates are missing and are currently being compiled.

# INVESTIGATIONS AND JURISDICTION ON NATIVE AMERICAN RESERVATIONS

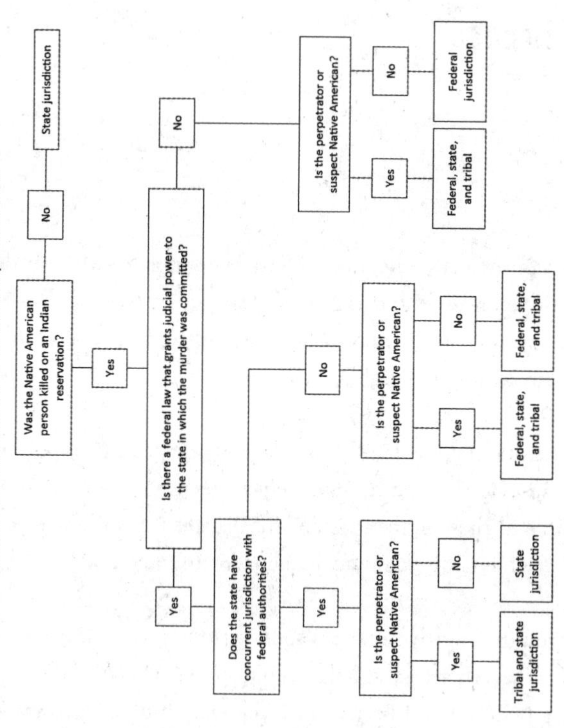

# Sources

This investigation would not have been possible without the victims' families and the trust they put in me. We met in the spring of 2024 on the Blackfeet and Northern Cheyenne territories and throughout Montana.

The stories told by family and friends are especially important because none of the law enforcement agencies agreed to speak with me. The FBI, the BIA, and the Blackfeet Law Enforcement all declined or ignored my requests for an interview.

Through lengthy conversations with activists, journalists, and researchers, I was able to confirm what the families had long believed and better grasp the magnitude of this crisis. All quotes come either from firsthand interviews or from excerpts from the sources listed below. Payne Lindsey's work was one of my most valuable resources in learning about each suspect's side of the story.

**Documentary Films and Podcasts**

Benally, Razelle and Matthew Galkin. *Murder in Big Horn.* Showtime Documentary, 2023.

"Episode 38: Kimberly HeavyRunner Loring." *I Am Interchange*, 2019. Podcast: https://iaminterchange.com/episode-38-kimberly-heavyrunner-loring/.

"Indigenous Student's Disappearance Part of Epidemic of Missing Native Women," ABC News video, 2019, https://abcnews.go.com/Nightline/video/indigenous-students-disappearance-part-epidemic-missing-native-women-66153570.

LaCour, Alice and Brett Talley. "The Disappearance of Ashley Loring HeavyRunner." *Prosecutors* Podcast: https://prosecutorspodcast.com/2023/06/06/194-the-disappearance-of-ashley-loring-heavyrunner-ninixksini/ Episode 194, 2023.

Landon, Christopher. *Never Seen Again: Ashley Loring HeavyRunner.* Paramount Plus, 2022.

Lappas, Kristen and Tom Rinaldi. *Blackfeet Boxing: Not Invisible.* ESPN documentary, 2020.

Leclaire, Tai. *The Truth Behind the Legend of Pocahontas.* PBS, 2023.

Lindsey, Payne. "The Disappearance of Ashley Loring HeavyRunner." Produced by Tenderfoot TV. *Up and Vanished*, 2021. Podcast: https://upandvanished.com/.

**Articles**

Many articles published by the local media, such as the *Billings Gazette,* the *Great Falls Tribune*, and the *Missoulian*, and especially the work of journalist Nora Mabie.

Online *ICT News* articles.

Reporting by *The Guardian* and *Marie Claire US* on Ashley Loring HeavyRunner; by *The New York Times* on Selena Not Afraid; and by *NBC News* on Mexican cartels.

News stories from KRTV and KFBB.

Reporting by *Four Points Media*, a nonprofit media organization serving the Crow Nation.

**Reports and Academic Sources**

*Maze of Injustice.* Amnesty International, 2007.

*Missing and Murdered Indigenous Women and Girls Report.* Urban Indian Health Institute, 2017–2018.

*Missing and Murdered: Confronting the Silent Crisis in Indian Country.* Oversight hearing before the Committee on Indian Affairs, US Senate. Transcript from the session held December 12, 2018.

*Looping in Native Communities.* Interim report to the State Tribal Relations Interim Committee, 2020.

*To' Kee Skuy' Soo Ney-Wo-Chek', (I Will See You Again in a Good Way).* Yurok Tribal Court and Sovereign Bodies Institute, 2020–2022.

**Books**

Deer, Sarah. *The Beginning and End of Rape: Confronting Sexual Violence in Native America.* University of Minnesota Press, 2015.

Dunbar-Ortiz, Roxanne. *An Indigenous Peoples' History of the United States.* Beacon Press, 2014.

Welch, James. *Killing Custer: The Battle of the Little Bighorn and the Fate of the Plains Indians.* W. W. Norton & Company, 1994.

**Further Information**

The NIRWC (National Indigenous Women's Resource Center) website: https://www.niwrc.org.

**About justice on Native land:**

Erdrich, Louise. *The Round House.* HarperCollins, 2012.

Heska Wanbli Weiden, David. *Winter Counts.* Ecco, 2020.

**About life on Native reservations:**

Harjo, Sterlin and Taika Waititi. *Reservation Dogs.* FX Hulu, 2021–2023.

**About the MMIW crisis in Quebec:**

Walter, Emmanuelle. *Stolen Sisters: The Story of Two Missing Girls, Their Families and How Canada Has Failed Indigenous Women.* Translated by Susan Ouriou. HarperCollins Publishers, 2015.

**About Montana's fifth season:**

Bass, Rick. *The Wild Marsh: Four Seasons at Home in Montana.* Houghton Mifflin Harcourt, 2009.

**Additional Comments**

Working on the MMIW crisis and the Ashley Loring HeavyRunner case gave me a glimpse into the darker aspects of life on reservations, these territories that are deprived of justice. But it's important to highlight that they are also places of resistance and spirituality, places that have borne scores of environmental activists, athletes, boxers, rodeo champions, and artists. As writer David Treuer once wrote in *Rez Life,* "What one finds on reservations is more than scars, tears, blood, and noble sentiment. There is beauty in Indian life. . . . We love our reservations."

Throughout this work, I used the words "Native," "Native American," and "Indigenous," as is customary in the United States. The term "Indian" was only included when quoting speakers who employed the term or who defined themselves as such. As much as possible, I avoided calling people living in the United States "American," as many Indigenous populations throughout the Americas are sensitive to the use of this word.

As of the completion of the translation, a $50,000 reward was still being offered for any information that might help locate Ashley Loring HeavyRunner.

# Acknowledgments

There aren't enough thank-yous to honor the strength of the women who agreed to meet with me despite the trauma and tears these interviews always bring up. I am grateful to Loxie Loring and Kimberly Loring HeavyRunner and to the women of the Blackfeet MMIP group: Rhonda Grant-Connelly, Wilma Fleury, Carlene Oldperson and her daughter Taco, and Paula Castro in Lame Deer.

Some difficult editorial decisions had to be made, and certain interviews and names of victims were omitted from the story. Every meeting and interview was a precious contribution, helping me understand the crisis and the repetition that defines this pattern of impunity. With that in mind, I especially wish to thank:

Bettina Tallbull, mother of Kayanna Gonzales, who was shot to death in front of her family in Billings in 2019.

Darlene Limberhand, mother of Deanna Fay Limberhand, who was found drowned in a river in Absarokee in 2021.

Sherri Ewing, mother of Arshanda KnowsHisGun, who was found drowned in a canal in Lockwood in 2022.

Ann Marceau, wife of Jamie Takes Gun, who was found dead in Great Falls in 2022.

Charles Upham, father of Misty Upham, who was found dead in Seattle in 2014.

And thank you to all the families I spoke with at the MMIP event in Missoula, held in March 2024: Carissa HeavyRunner, Mika Westwolf's mother; Yolanda Fraser, Kaysera Stops Pretty Places's grandmother; and Valenda Morigeau, Jermain Charlo's auntie.

May you see justice served.

I would also like to highlight the enormous work of activists in the movement, who face traumatic stories daily and have often been personally affected by the crisis. Erica Shelby, Haley Omeasoo, Theresa Small, Ivan MacDonald, and Charlene Sleeper, the founder of MMIP Billings, all patiently spoke with me at length to help me understand the movement, which is still in its infancy. I hope I was able to accurately capture the issues you are fighting for. None of this would have been possible without help from Annita Hetoevehotohke'e Lucchesi—I will never forget the moving ceremony organized by Cheyenne singers to honor the memory of Arshanda KnowsHisGun, near Lame Deer.

In the Blackfeet community, Frankie Kipp, founder of the Blackfeet Nation Boxing Club, and his wife Ember Kipp were the first people to welcome me on the reservation and invite me out to dinner at the Browning casino. Robert Desrosier, a key supporter of the MMIP group, introduced me to the Blackfeet Tribal Council. My discussion with the employees of the Blackfeet Tribal Preservation Office was also an important introduction to the history of the tribe.

Diana Burd, daughter of Diana Burd, has also done tremendous work in searching for victims and has contributed to improving legislation. Her mother provided valuable information about the Blackfeet language and culture.

Thank you to Cary Lance, AKA White Buffalo, for agreeing to meet with me in Billings.

I've already touched on the importance of Payne Lindsey's work, but I'm also grateful that he took the time to answer my questions while he was busy with new investigative fieldwork. Journalists Rachel CrowSpreadingWings and Luella Brien were immensely helpful as well.

The following people also provided valuable insights into the crisis: Dana Toole, head of the Special Services Bureau in the Division of Criminal Investigation of the Montana Department of Justice; Elisa Fiaschetti, program director at the Montana Community Foundation, which manages the Snowbird Fund; and Lowell Hochhalter, the cofounder of The Lifeguard Group.

In January 2023, I wrote a story for *Society* magazine about two Native American women, Emmilee Risling and Khadijah Britton, who are still missing in Northern California. My interviews with their loved ones, as well as with Dr. Blythe K. George, Chief Judge Abby Abinanti, and Tribal Police Chief Greg O'Rourke, were the starting point for my reporting on the MMIW crisis. Thank you for opening this door for me.

Thanks to Linda for making me feel at home in Billings, to Lauren for her hospitality in Missoula, and to Melissa for an evening spent at the legendary Sip 'n Dip in Great Falls.

And because we shared a lot of laughs to get through it all and because the Blackfeet MMIP girls asked me to add this story: Thanks to the Glacier County police officer who let me off with a warning for speeding in what was surely the funniest car chase in Highway 2 history.

Thank you to my family and friends for their unwavering support, and especially my parents, Léa and Coline, who are now used to proofreading my work and dealing with my brainstorming sessions.

I want to honor the memory of Mélanie Houé—a passionate journalist who inspired many careers and a friend gone too soon.

Last but not least, thank you to Stéphane Régy for his sharp eye, continued trust, and the space he carves out in *Society* magazine for my obsessions, and to Elsa Delachair who, beyond being a talented editor, knew how to bolster my confidence throughout the investigation and writing process with the same energy she brings to the ring.

## About the Author

Anaïs Renevier is a French journalist. She regularly travels the United States to cover communities living on the margins of society. To deliver in-depth stories, she has spent time engaging with the Proud Boys in Miami, undocumented cannabis workers in California, and reclusive hippies in remote parts of Hawai'i. She also regularly writes about Indigenous communities across North America. Renevier is the author of *The Alice Crimmins Case*, an investigation into a mother pitted against the patriarchal American justice system. When she is not working as a journalist and author, she freelances as a florist and enjoys boxing. She lives in Marseille, France.

# CRIME INK PRESENTS

**FRANCE'S LEADING TRUE CRIME JOURNALISTS INVESTIGATE AMERICA'S MOST NOTORIOUS CASES — ONE FOR EVERY STATE IN THE UNION.**

Each title revisits an infamous crime, replete with all the hard facts and gruesome details, and brings fresh new perspectives to these storied cases. Taken together, the series reveals a dark national legacy, state-by-state from sea to shining sea . . .

## NEW YORK: THE ALICE CRIMMINS CASE

**ANAÏS RENEVIER**

**TRANSLATED BY LAURIE BENNETT**

**ISBN: 978-1-61316-629-1**

The case that rocked New York City in the summer of ′65. Two children disappear and turn up dead. Their beautiful and promiscuous mother is convicted in the court of public opinion . . . but did she commit the crime?

## CALIFORNIA: THE GOLDEN STATE KILLER CASE

**WILLIAM THORP**

**TRANSLATED BY LYNN E. PALERMO**

**ISBN: 978-1-61316-631-4**

For years a methodical killer stalked the shadows of sunny California. Responsible for at least fifty assaults and thirteen murders, an unlikely modern development led to an arrest more than forty years after his reign of terror began.

## OHIO: THE CLEVELAND JOHN DOE CASE

**THIBAULT RAISSE**

**TRANSLATED BY LAURIE BENNETT**

**ISBN: 978-1-61316-633-8**

A body is discovered by police in 2002 . . . but it doesn't match its name. The deceased had assumed a false identity. Who was he really? And what other secrets was he hiding?

## MISSISSIPPI: THE EMMETT TILL CASE

**JEAN-MARIE POTTIER**

**TRANSLATED BY LYNN PALERMO**

**ISBN: 978-1-61316-692-5**

In August 1955, the lifeless and disfigured body of a teenager was fished out of the Tallahatchie River in Mississippi. The body was that of Emmett Till, a fourteen-year-old Black boy from Chicago who had come to spend vacation with his mother's family.

## SOUTH CAROLINA: THE MURDAUGH MURDERS CASE

**ARTHUR CERF**

**TRANSLATED BY LYNN E. PALERMO**

**ISBN: 978-1-61316-694-9**

For the first time in his life, attorney Alex Murdaugh stands before a jury at the Colleton Courthouse, not as a practitioner of law, but rather as a defendant, having been accused of murdering both his wife Maggie and his son Paul.

## WASHINGTON, DC: THE CHANDRA LEVY CASE

**HÉLÈNE COUTARD**

**TRANSLATED BY LAURIE BENNETT**

**ISBN: 978-1-61316-696-3**

The disappearance of Chandra Levy had everything: exposure of the love lives of politicians; a young, white victim. The investigation gave way to outlandish theories. Was the government involved? Was there a cover-up? And what would that mean for American politics?